CLAIMING YOUR PLACE

AT THE

BOARDROOM TABLE

THE ESSENTIAL HANDBOOK
FOR EXCELLENCE IN GOVERNANCE AND
EFFECTIVE DIRECTORSHIP

THOMAS BAKEWELL
JAMES J. DARAZSDI

Mc
Graw
Hill
Education

New York   Chicago   San Francisco   Athens   London
Madrid   Mexico City   Milan   New Delhi
Singapore   Sydney   Toronto

1 2 3 4 5 6 7 8 9 0   2QVD/QVS   1 2 0 9 8 7 6 5 4

ISBN   978-0-07-183358-5
MHID   0-07-183358-7

e-ISBN   978-0-07-183359-2
e-MHID   0-07-183359-5

Library of Congress Cataloging-in-Publication Data
Bakewell, Thomas, 1953-
    Claiming your place at the boardroom table : the essential handbook for excellence in governance and effective directorship / by Thomas Bakewell.
        pages cm
        ISBN 978-0-07-183358-5 (hardback) — ISBN 0-07-183358-7 (hardback)
1. Boards of directors.   2. Corporate governance.   I. Title.
    HD2745.B224 2015
    658.4'22—dc23

                                                        2014021886

McGraw-Hill Education books are available at special quantity discounts to use as premiums and sales promotions, or for use in corporate training programs. To contact a representative, please visit the Contact Us page at www.mhprofessional.com.

James J. Darazsdi worked tirelessly over the course of three decades to improve the governance of the many boards and institutions for which he served as a director, executive, and teacher. His governance wisdom, business pragmatism, and financial expertise shaped literally thousands of corporate leaders over the span of his impressive career as a business and academic leader. I am privileged to carry his legacy forward in this book.

—*Thomas Bakewell*

❖ ❖ ❖

Recognizing the Achievements of Dr. James "Jim" Darazsdi

"Darazsdi's experience in a wide variety of companies, both large and small, privately held and public, from food processing to bridge building made him a valuable contributor. His thoughts expressed through his writings in many publications and his books are most worthy of our attention."

Richard Hardy
Chairman Emeritus, Affinity Group, Inc.

"Dr. Darazsdi was a strong advocate for Good Governance, and he dedicated most of his time practicing and teaching good corporate governance practices. And today, Dr. Darazsdi's book is a crowning jewel from his numerous years of work on such an important topic, and I am confident that it will be used and adopted as a reference manual by companies and institutions worldwide."

Antoine N. "Tony" Frem
Chairman of the Board,
Interstate Resources Inc. Vice Chairman of Board
INDEVCO Group and Mayor of the city of Jounieh – Lebanon

"I think of the wisdom [Darazsdi] brings to the field of leadership and hope that his 'legacy' textbook can truly portray his wonderful contributions."

William C. "Bill" Crews, PhD,
Executive Director, Nonpublic Postsecondary Education Commission

"Through his research while working on his doctoral dissertation, and afterward, Jim became an expert on corporate boards and the qualities needed to become a board member and to add value to a company. This book will be must-reading for business students or for anyone considering becoming a board director."

Marcie Harris, MBA Director of Administration
Raymond James Financial Services, Inc. Member FINRA/SIPC

"James Darazsdi came into a struggling nonprofit and provided his business skills to get Nichols College back on track. Jim brought a fresh look to the College from an industry perspective, which began to refocus Nichols on its core operations."

Debra M. Townsley, PhD
President, William Peace University

"Jim's association with the National Association of Corporate Directors provided valuable insights into how he could improve our own board performance. Jim developed the board charter and the annual evaluation of board performance, both of which are used today."

Jim Perdue
Owner, Perdue Farms

"Jim Darazsdi was an outstanding chief financial officer of Rocco Inc."

Robert H. "Twig" Strickler
Rocco Enterprises Owner

CONTENTS

Foreword

The Path to the Boardroom

People often ask if I can help them get on a board of directors, which goes with the territory as an officer of the National Association of Corporate Directors (NACD). Few people, though, know what it actually takes to be a director—especially on a public company board. Gone are the days of the 1980s when a board seat was more of an honorary position. The events of the past 15 to 20 years have put a new lens on board service, and to paraphrase Bob Dylan, "The times—they have a changed." Still, board service has a lot to offer, but it takes a lot in return.

When I started my career at NACD, I was introduced to Jim Darazsdi. Jim had a unique blend of experiences, from academic, to CEO, to board member of a variety of companies, public, private, and nonprofit. Most importantly, Jim was a lifelong student and someone who truly believed that everyone could benefit from continuous learning. At the time I met Jim, he was the "chair emeritus" of NACD, and although he was no longer on our board, he remained very active with NACD—most prominently on our faculty, teaching everything from finance to strategy. I had the pleasure to work with him for about 8 years until I received a phone call from him indicating that he was writing a book—as his legacy. He told me he was dying and only had a few months to live, but he wanted to leave a book to help inform the next generation of students of governance and board service. Shortly thereafter, Jim's wife Janet called to tell me Jim had passed. She sent me his manuscript and asked if I could help her get it finished—and published. I called the only person I thought might be able to build on the solid foundation that Jim had started—Tom Bakewell.

Tom took up the challenge, and today, you are the beneficiary. Tom has put together a thoughtful and well-structured guide to board service, with interviews of serving directors, case studies to bring examples to life, and down-to-earth practical guidance to help those at the top of their games understand what it will take to move to the next level and serve a company on its board of directors. He chose the title carefully—*Claiming Your Place*—not that you are entitled to it, but that you will need to demonstrate excellence in governance and board leadership to maintain that claim. He dispels some common myths about board service, advises the reader of the time commitments of both seeking a seat and of actual service once a seat is attained, and then walks through the basics of what it takes to demonstrate excellence.

Claiming Your Place brings users real-life examples to illustrate the many nuances of board service. The pages are filled with discussions of legal cases, reporting requirements, regulatory descriptions and enforcements, and the overarching fiduciary duties of directors. Following the Darazsdi lead, Tom weaves in some basics of finance, discusses the roles of the key board committees, then dives into strategy and risk, and comes full circle to address the current environment with proxy advisory firms and new federal laws that are fundamentally changing how boards operate today. For any student of the game, aspiring director, or even for serving directors who need a comprehensive overview of the landscape in which they are operating, Tom Bakewell has provided you with all of the steps to consider when walking the path.

—Peter Gleason
Managing Director and CFO, NACD,
National Association of Corporate Directors

ACKNOWLEDGMENTS

A special thanks to Alexandra Lajoux and Janet Darazsdi for making this project happen. Thanks for your steadfast commitment to Jim's legacy, my efforts, and the world of governance. And thanks to James Darazsdi for his many contributions to governance and the NACD.

To Zachary Gajewski, thanks for the personal touch and your great expertise in bringing this dream and book to fruition.

For giving me true encouragement, thanks to Mike Weinberg and Carol Weisman.

For sharing years of talent with me, thanks to Richard Weiss, Laura Stanton, and David LaGesse. For getting me started thanks to Jennifer Stolzer. For providing great support from start to finish, thanks to Matt Belz.

For the opportunity to grow my experience in governance with world-class peers thanks to the entire team of the NACD, and especially Steve Walker, Erin Essenmacher, and Chelsea Moody.

Most importantly, thanks to my amazing bride Julia. You make life fun, a great journey, and new challenges possible.

Introduction

Claiming Your Place at the Boardroom Table

It has been said that governance is a journey, a conversation, and a shared experience to be lived out with your colleagues. Those are all apt descriptions. And it is more.

Governance, especially corporate governance involving the oversight of an organization by a board of directors, is a fascinating field. For many, what takes place in the boardroom with a board of directors overseeing the company has always involved a bit of mystery, a lot of complexity, and even excitement and drama now and then. It can also involve lots of important but routine hard work that requires building relationships, solving problems, meshing personalities, growing leadership teams, managing power struggles, and handling crises.

Corporate governance has evolved for many decades. During that time some parts have changed little. But since 2000, a great deal has changed dramatically and affected private companies, nonprofits and public companies around the world.

A superb March 2014 Harvard Business Review article, "The Boardroom's Quiet Revolution," highlights many of the changes. These include:

▶ Public company regulations that require a majority of directors be independent

▶ Active use of a lead or presiding independent director when a joint chairman and CEO are involved

▶ Regular executive sessions of the independent directors only without the CEO present

▶ Audit committees with far more responsibility and accountability

And those are just a few. They are all covered here along with many more.

Many believe the first real breakthrough in America's corporate boardrooms came with a coup at General Motors in 1992. GM chairman John Smale ousted CEO Bob Stempel with the help of outside directors. GM was faced with high costs, being slow to market and massive bureaucracy. The board sought change, and Stempel had resisted.

Prior to this GM coup, the word "imperial" described many CEOs. It was common for the CEO to select the directors and they would serve at his pleasure.

As a second act, GM directors in 1994 established a set of operating Board Guidelines on Significant Corporate Governance Issues leading with the concept of a separate chairman and CEO, adding the independent lead director concept, and much more.

Today, we have the successor General Motors Company Board of Directors Corporate Governance Guidelines, a list of 38 governance guidelines covering 15 pages. The first question many ask about good governance is "What are the 'best practices' to follow?" Best practices are covered extensively in this book.

How This Book Can Help

This volume provides the road map and resources for both seasoned and first time directors to become knowledgeable and effective board members. It is a handbook that describes the processes, tools, and techniques they can use to achieve excellence in governance.

Chapter 1 covers joining your first board. "Can you ask to join a board?" is a common question for those new to governance. Conventional wisdom says no. You must be invited. But there are exceptions. The opportunities and ways that work are covered in depth.

Chapters 2 and 3 focus on the basics of being an effective director and the ways a board does its work to achieve excellence in governance overall. You will benefit from my own experience. My first board service was fun and smooth sailing. I benefited from great leadership, and learned a lot. My second board looked perfect from the outside, but was a train wreck in every way possible. I soon butted heads with a truly delightful but totally imperial chairman of the board. Rome was burning and yet every board meeting was scripted to the minute with monologue, speaking up was unheard of, and not a moment of true dialogue took place. We learned the hard way why "going concern" audit opinions can kill your line of credit, lead to immediate crisis, and dozens of other lessons that can only come from a baptism by fire.

After a decade of heavy lifting on my part and many others on the board, a sleepy tradition-bound organization on death's door went from life support to robust health with annual revenues that grew from $8 million to $90 million including enviable margins and earnings. That board and management team learned about exemplary directorship, and I became committed to good governance in a passionate way.

Must you be financially literate to serve on a board? Do you have to know the alphabet soup of laws affecting public companies today to safely serve on any type of board? Chapter 4 explores important topics related to boards and finance including personal financial literacy. Chapter 5 covers what you need to know about public company reporting.

Chapters 6 and 7 pull all the pieces together for directors and boards to achieve excellence in governance, and to learn from the experiences of others.

Join me in plumbing the depths of good governance with *Claiming Your Place at the Boardroom Table: The Essential Handbook for Excellence in Governance and Effective Directorship.* May your journey into good governance be both personally satisfying and professionally rewarding.

YOUR FIRST BOARD

Insightful authors aim their books not just at anyone, but for a particular audience. If you are in this audience, you already are successful. You have climbed the corporate ladder at your company or started a prosperous business of your own. Over the years, you have acquired skills, taken risks, and probably made a few mistakes. But overall you have gained the trust and confidence of your colleagues and superiors.

You have a lot to offer. You are looking for a new challenge.

The next step for you may be a seat at the boardroom table. This book is aimed at getting you there, and then helping you become the most effective and honorable board member that you can be. Reading along with you will be seasoned directors and students of corporate governance. They should find it a useful guide to governance and a means for reviewing foundational concepts and keeping up-to-date with best practices.

Board service is a calling that can provide enormous satisfaction, whether you are signing on with a nonprofit or taking a seat at the pinnacle of the corporate world as one of the 200 to 300 people each year who claim a seat at a Standard & Poor's (S&P's) 500 company.

FIGURE 1.1 What is the Time Commitment?

	Nonprofit	Private	Public
Number of full board meetings per year	6.2	5.3	5.4
Average number of hours per meeting	4.5	5.3	6.6
Average total hours spent per year Includes attending meetings, traveling to/from board events, reviewing reports and other materials, director education, and representing the organization at public events.	163.4	180.1	235.9

Time commitments vary by the type of board.

Source: National Association of Corporate Directors, Annual Surveys, 2013–2014.

You are sure to learn a great deal along the way, and if your board is typical, you can expect to spend 200 to 300 hours each year fulfilling your duties (see Figure 1.1).

The rewards of board service can be substantial. They include:

▶ Acquiring knowledge on a wide range of topics in a specific industry or professional field.

▶ Making top new professional contacts.

▶ Contributing in meaningful ways to the growth of the company you serve.

▶ Developing leadership skills in the boardroom that serve others and benefit you.

▶ Launching you and your career in new, often surprising, directions and arenas.

If the board seat is with a nonprofit or charity, the director pay, with some exceptions, is usually negligible or nonexistent, so you will need to seek your rewards and satisfaction from addressing a community need and perhaps earning some modest recognition. You can certainly expect to be asked to make financial contributions to support the mission in addition to your hard work. But recognize, too, the many intangible benefits that come from nonprofit service. Your hard work can lead to more professional relationships, in general, and future board opportunities, in particular.

If you have achieved a paid board seat, work doubly hard to earn your pay and develop your boardroom skills. Your performance can lead to offers and invitations to serve on more boards, perhaps even including an S&P 500 company board. Those positions provided average director compensation in excess of $242,000 annually according to the *Spencer Stuart Board Index 2012*. Committee and board chairs earned even more.

Board pay and the related rewards can vary widely, but the vast majority of directors find board service challenging, interesting, and satisfying no matter the rate of pay.

How Do You Find That First Seat at the Boardroom Table?

If you are looking to join your first board, and are eager for the answers now, here is a top-line summary of effective approaches for gaining a boardroom seat, shown in Figure 1.2. You will want to keep reading subsequent chapters for in-depth information and methods for securing board seats and becoming a skilled director.

We will carefully review here a number of proven approaches. We will also illuminate the concepts by providing true stories about

FIGURE 1.2 Ways to Connect to a Board Seat

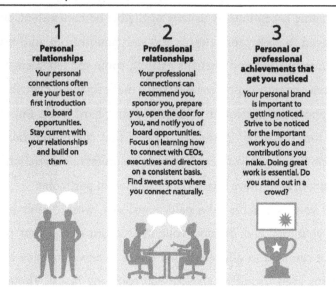

how talented people landed their seats at the boardroom table. For some, it was their first board seat and for others, it was that long-sought-out and coveted board seat of their dreams.

There are three top approaches to gaining a boardroom seat. The first is no big secret.

Your Connections with Personal Relationships

Poll any size group of serving directors and 60 to 70 percent or more will consistently tell you that their board seat came from someone they know having them in mind and acting on their behalf. Add to that the possibility of securing a board seat through someone you know putting you in touch with someone he or she knows and the number skyrockets.

Ideally, you are a people person who has an active plan to grow and cultivate your personal and business relationships. If you are not a people person, then all the more reason to have a plan to grow and cultivate your personal and business relationships that can move you steadily toward your goal of landing a boardroom seat.

Your Connections with Professional Relationships

Start with people you know and let them know of your interest and qualifications for board service. Be sure you take the time to learn, through genuine interest and caring, their backgrounds, experience, and stories. Inevitably, if you take the time to go deeper with your professional relationships, you will be surprised with what you learn about how the world is connected. My early personal experience with being intentional about knowing my professional connections better revealed a funny accountant from Saturday morning tennis who was chief financial officer (CFO) of a leading worldwide hospitality company. It also revealed a quiet fellow from church who appeared to have a baby picture franchise at the local hospital when in reality he owned the nation's largest firm in that industry. One connected me to my first board in public broadcasting and the other opened the door for a local college board seat.

Next, *fish where the fish are.* That old expression speaks the truth. If you want to be on boards you are advised to fish where the fish are. That means reaching out, connecting with and getting to know current board members and chief executive officers (CEOs).

If you are serious about finding boardroom seats, the highest and best use of your time is connecting with the people currently in the boardroom. As you would expect, building these relationships takes a great deal of time.

But let me add that fishing where the fish are can go far beyond just knowing and connecting with the people currently in the boardroom. It can include and encompass dozens of approaches. Here are just three:

- Knowing and connecting with the people headed into the boardroom—like talented executives on the rise or busy young entrepreneurs and professionals.
- Researching new opportunities that might be developing in the days ahead—like an old board looking to add new blood, or a start-up seeking a particular talent, or a major company spinning off a new division and building a board from scratch.
- Finding a tiny ad in your hometown newspaper announcing elections for the local school board, or the *Wall Street Journal* seeking recommendations or applicants to fill a boardroom seat for a privately held business, a major public organization, or a well-known national charity.

Your Personal Brand

In succeeding with your work and job, talent counts and talent wins, time and again. And so it is with boards seeking new talent to fill the next boardroom seat. Recruiters seek and select those people who are getting noticed. Getting noticed includes:

- Being identified as the best or extraordinary for what you do when people you know or serve with are asked to give a reference for you or talk to someone about you.
- Having strong skills and talents in a specific area that the board is seeking at a particular moment like sales, finance, or technology. Those with operating experience, experience

running something, and having profit-and-loss responsibility, routinely have an edge.

▶ Having a proven record of making good decisions, using good judgment, and being supportive of the team in your work.

▶ Showing character, integrity, and leadership in good times or bad in all you do.

In the following chapter you will find true stories about how others landed their first seats at the boardroom table, some from sterling networking skills, and others from myriad approaches including research, career success, competitive application, and other surprising ways.

Of course, when you do your networking and begin talking with board recruiters, you want to sound like you know what you are talking about, even if it's your first board seat.

So let's take a quick look now at the key topics of governance, types of board opportunities, and what it takes to be a director.

WHAT IS GOVERNANCE?

"Governance" is one of those commonly used terms that many use but few can clearly define.

My favorite definition of governance comes from a seasoned corporate director who has spent years serving on global corporate boards. She says, "Governance is a conversation." By this I believe she means that governance is evolving, growing, and changing to meet the current needs and demands of modern-day organizations.

My own definition says, "Governance is experiential and reality based." What is the matter at hand that we need to attend to and how is it best addressed? It means governance is very much learned over time from taking the many theories and good ideas of governance and applying them to the current circumstances and reality. The substance and form of good governance is stimulating and interesting, but it is in the real world of application where the rubber hits the road. The best lessons are learned over time.

Nothing More Challenging

"There is one thing all boards have in common . . . they do not function."

Those are the words of the legendary consultant Peter Drucker.[1]

If I might parse Drucker's words, the boards of his day (the latter third of the twentieth century) actually did function, just not very well. That is to say, directors showed up, directors' fees were paid, meetings were held, corporate formalities were attended to, and business was conducted. But in the early 1970s, it was a time of the imperial CEO when boards routinely served at the pleasure of their CEOs and did their bidding. These stories are common and include the one of a renowned U.S. Steel CEO who when asked what he would do if the board did not approve his latest merger, retorted that he would get a new board.

Of course, this approach flies in the face of how all this is supposed to work. So let's review the basics.

Corporations are generally owned and controlled by their stockholders, stakeholders, or members or the corporation. The stockholders elect directors. Directors of a corporation, and not the shareholders, govern and manage the business and affairs of the corporation.

It's as simple as 1-2-3:

1. Stockholders elect directors.
2. Directors appoint and oversee management.
3. Management handles the day-to-day operations of the corporation.

So corporate governance is simple, straightforward, and easy, right?

Yes, except for micromanagement, when boards get in the way of managers doing their jobs. Except when board members fail to properly perform their duties in providing oversight. Except when the operations do not work. Except when the stockholders, directors, or management do not agree or get along. Except for the endless number of matters and concerns that get in the way of oversight and day-to-day operations of the corporation. And so forth.

The good news is that in the decades since Drucker spoke of nonfunctioning boards many have buckled down and done prodigious amounts of work, research, and study on the related topics of corporate governance, directors, boards, management, leadership, and more. Their leadership created a great deal of positive change in boardrooms worldwide.

Lawmakers pitched in as well. They have passed the Foreign Corrupt Practices Act (FCPA) of 1977, the Sarbanes-Oxley Act (SOX) of 2002, and the Dodd-Frank Wall Street Reform and Consumer Protection Act of 2010 (Dodd-Frank Act). This has led to even more change in the boardroom.

Most importantly, an entire community of people and organizations have become vitally interested in corporate governance and the high calling of pursuing good corporate governance. They share the view that boards, boardrooms, and corporations can function in a positive and productive manner with good leadership, guidance, and information.

Types of Board Opportunities

In the United States alone, there are millions (yes millions) of board positions, with hundreds of thousands of board positions opening annually.

We can group organizations with boards into four categories:

1. Private companies
2. Charities and nonprofits
3. Publicly traded companies
4. Government and quasi-government agencies

Here is a summary based on several good resources, along with a quick comparison chart in Figure 1.3:

1. **Private companies.** As of 2008, there were 27,281,452 "firms" or business entities in the United States according to the U.S. census. The vast majority of these would be privately held and owned companies. If you subtract the partnerships, sole proprietorships, and nonprofit entities, you have some 10 million private companies.[2]
2. **Charities and nonprofits.** Estimates from 2012 put the number of charities and nonprofits in the United States in excess of 1.5 million, including some 950,000 public charities, nearly 100,000 private foundations, and some 500,000 other special entities like mutual insurance companies, state-chartered credit unions, and cooperative-type associations or entities.[3]

FIGURE 1.3 Comparison of Types of Boards

	Public Company	Private Company	Charity, Nonprofit	Government Agency*
Entity definition:	A company that has issued securities through an initial public offering and is publicly traded.	A company whose ownership is private (i.e., not governmental, publicly traded).	A company that uses its profits to improve its services.	An entity that is owned, controlled, or supported by federal, state, or local governments.
Number of entities in the U.S.:	5,000 active with up to 20,000 registered	Tens of millions	1,537,465	Tens of thousands
Examples:	Citigroup Inc.	A physician group	Salvation Army	A school district
Overarching goal of board:	Generates profits for shareholders.	Generates profits for owners/accomplish owners' personal and social goals.	Fulfills a mission of service to constituency.	Not to make a profit, but to accomplish a public mission.
Typical board size:	Median size of 7 to 9.	Generally small with 3 to 4, up to 7 or 8 at larger companies.	Median size of 17, but often quite large (as many as 40 or 50).	Wide-ranging depending on size of government
Membership:	Primary owners, business executives, or other professionals.	Primary owners, business executives, or other professionals.	Variety of people from business, government, and voluntary sectors.	Variety of people from business, government, and voluntary sectors.
Public accountability:	Extensive regulatory review of SEC, Stock Exchanges, and myriad agencies/laws.	Very little.	Extensive, providing reports, and making activities widely known.	Moderate with IRS Tax Exemption, state Attorneys General/agencies driving reporting. Heavy fund raising requires strong accountability.
Primary beneficiaries:	Shareholders.	Private owners.	Customers/users of nonprofit's service.	The public.
Term of Office:	Many have term limits.	Often no term limits.	Many have term limits.	Often elected or appointed by office holders with regular term limits.
Compensation:	Often paid nice combination of cash fees and some stock awards.	Often paid modest cash fees.	Rarely paid cash, some pay modest education or expenses. A handful do pay.	Rarely paid, with a few paying nicely.

*Includes quasi-governmental agencies.

Source: National Association of Corporate Directors for board size annual surveys; news reports.

Depending on the type of board, experiences will differ. Some are paid, some are not. Some have term limits, others do not. Here is a general comparison of the characteristics by type of board.

3. **Publicly traded companies.** The 2013 Credit Risk Monitor "Directory of Public Companies in the United States" lists 21,650 public companies operating among the various 50 states and has information available on over 40,000 publicly traded companies, with a total count of over 80,000 public companies worldwide.

4. **Government and quasi-government agencies.** The number of government and quasi-government agencies is vast. Suffice to say that in most major metropolitan areas and state capitals, there are hundreds of agencies providing opportunities for board service.

Two points of clarification. First, there will be other entities that fall beyond these four groups. Examples include a large number of religious orders, fraternities, and sororities.

Second, some organizations can fall outside of these four groups or are included in more than one group. For example, there is a large group of entities known as nongovernmental organizations (NGOs). Generally, they are nonprofits that can have substantial government funding, so they have characteristics of both nonprofits and quasi-governmental agencies. The United States is estimated to have well over a million NGOs.

There are a wide range of legal and organizational structures, including:

- The Sole Proprietorship
- Partnerships of all kinds, including general, limited, and special purpose
- Joint Ventures

- ▶ Associations
- ▶ Trusts and Business Trusts
- ▶ Corporations
- ▶ Professional Corporations
- ▶ Limited Liability Corporations
- ▶ Special Purpose Corporations
- ▶ Subsidiaries or divisions of any of these entities

With those caveats in mind, let's return to our four general types of business entities that provide board opportunities.

Private Companies

A *private company* is owned by individuals or partners and is not publicly traded. Private companies can range from old-fashioned sole proprietors involving an owner and no employees to partnerships with a handful of owners or employees to major private companies known worldwide with more than 100,000 employees.

Sole proprietorship examples:

- ▶ Tutor
- ▶ Landscaper
- ▶ Mechanic

Partnership examples:

- ▶ Law firms
- ▶ Physician groups
- ▶ Some accounting firms

Limited liability company examples:

- ► Chrysler Group LLC, the automobile manufacturer
- ► Pricewaterhouse Coopers LLP, among the Big Four accounting firms
- ► Mrs. Fields Famous Brands, LLC, the cookie company

Private corporation examples:

- ► Mars, a candy and pet food manufacturer
- ► Publix Supermarkets
- ► Enterprise Rent-A-Car

Charities and Nonprofits

Charities and *nonprofits* are generally considered companies that do not operate for the primary purpose of making a profit for the benefit of any particular person or owner. They are owned for the benefit of some charitable or community purpose, and usually have a state or federal tax exempt status. Charities and nonprofits use any net gains and profits to improve services to their beneficiaries. These organizations can range from public charities to private foundations to mutual insurance companies to state-chartered credit unions, and cooperative-type associations or entities.

Public charity examples:

- ► The Salvation Army
- ► The United Way, both as a national organization and its many local chapters
- ► Most any of the local favorite charities you can think of, like the Animal Protective Association of Missouri, a favorite of mine

Private foundation examples:
- The J. Paul Getty Trust
- Bill and Melinda Gates Foundation
- Any number of smaller local private foundations you can think of in your community

There are several other types of special entities. Many of the Blue Cross and Blue Shield Plans in the United States operate as mutual insurance companies. Many of the large national member-owned companies like grower-run Ocean Spray or retailer-owned Ace Hardware or Rural Electric Cooperative Association are run as cooperatives. Also, there are many other types of special entities like national and state chartered-credit unions.

Publicly Traded Companies

A *publicly traded company* is a company that has issued securities to the general public through an initial public offering (IPO) and is traded on one of the public stock exchanges. Notable examples of publicly traded companies include the 5,000 or so major well-known public companies like McDonald's running restaurants, Coca-Cola Company selling beverages, and Boeing Company building airplanes.

Many public companies operate worldwide, like Citigroup with some 250,000 employees and more than $60 billion in annual revenue. Others are locally based with annual revenues in the $100 million range and have fewer employees.

Government and Quasi-Government Agencies

A *government agency* is an entity that is owned or controlled by federal, state, or local government. A *quasi-government agency* is an entity that is owned, sponsored, created by or supported by the government but managed privately.

Government agencies include state government, towns, and school districts to name just a few. Quasi-government agencies include widely known entities like Amtrak (National Railroad Passenger Corporation), Fannie Mae (Federal National Mortgage Association), and Farm Credit Banks.

Do Your Homework and Scope It Out

A key point to keep in mind when researching organizations for board seat opportunities is that organizational and legal structures can change over the years, and, at times, overnight. No matter the organizational structure, there are almost always ongoing or successor boardroom opportunities.

Huge public companies can go private like Michael Dell winning a high-stakes well-publicized battle to take Dell private after years as a public company. Some companies are like chameleons operating alternately between public and private depending on what their strategy, debt structures, or owners dictate.

Wall Street investment bankers are ever eager to take the next hot start-up through its initial public offering (IPO) whether it's the high-profile companies made into legends like Google, Facebook, and Twitter or the lesser-known, more mundane IPOs like beauty brand company Coty, or the Kelly Blue Book owners who built a billion-dollar company known as AutoTrader.com that has announced plans for an IPO one day soon.

Major nonprofits like many of the traditional Blue Cross Plans have after decades of operation converted from nonprofit to for-profit status or sold their companies' assets and operations to for-profit public companies. Typically, these corporate conversions then created large charitable foundations with the proceeds serving some community good like public health. In the process, they generated numerous new boardroom opportunities. And it is not uncommon for private companies to turn their efforts full tilt into charitable endeavors by converting their business operations into private foundations or not-for-profit charities, like a number of well-known colleges have done in recent years, such as the Savannah College of Art and Design (SCAD) in Georgia and Keiser University in Florida.

Here are estimates of board opportunities that might arise each year for each of the categories we've covered, with further information comparing them in Figure 1.4.

1. **Private companies: roughly 10 million seats each year.**
    Approximately 7 million private companies have directors with the average board size estimated as high as 7 directors.[4] In a survey of over 500 private companies, the National Association of Corporate Directors (NACD) found private company boards to average 7.3 directors. If one director turns over every 7 years, these companies would add 10 million directors per year.

2. **Charities and nonprofits: roughly 2 million nonprofit board seats need to be filled each year.** An estimated 1.8 million nonprofit board seats turn over annually.[5] Boards of nonprofits have high levels of turnover, with more than 80 percent replacing at least one director in 2012.[6]

3. **Publicly traded companies: roughly 20,000 public company board seats likely open each year.** More than 20,000 public companies do business in the United States with an average

FIGURE 1.4 How Many Opportunities Are Available for Board Service?

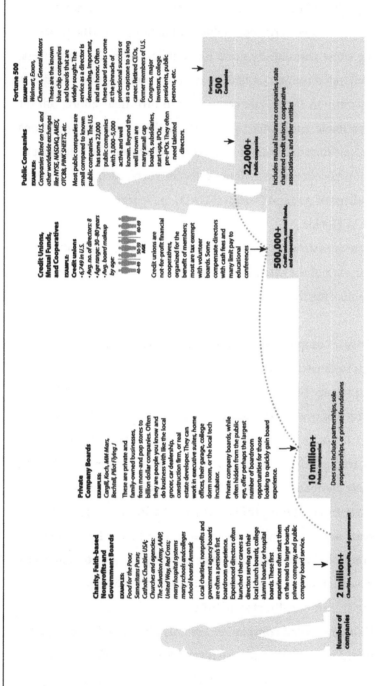

A surprisingly large number of boardroom opportunities exist. Exceptional individuals join boards in each of these five categories at any point in their career. Typically, service starts with a local charity or nonprofit board like your church, college, or hospital. Many progress up the stairs to more opportunities.

board size of 10.7 directors and a tenure of 8.6 years.[7] This suggests at least one director search per year on average.

4. **Government and quasi-government agencies: easily 100,000 government-related board seats open each year.** There are over 90,000 federal, state, and local government units and over 14,000 school systems according to the 2012 U.S. Census Bureau. When you include quasi-official agencies, private regulatory agencies, boards, commissions, chartered organizations, and more, the number grows.

What Does It Take to Become a Director?

The first steps to joining a board may require little more on your part than a mere expression of a willingness to serve. As a starting point, you need only to be named, invited, appointed, or elected to a board to claim your seat. Some might spend years seeking to join their first board of directors. For others, the opportunity to join their first board might show up unexpectedly, serendipitously, at a tender age, or even overnight.

I mentioned that there are three top approaches to gaining a boardroom seat. This upfront tip was meant to be direct and to encourage those rare birds who have the benefit of flying in the rarified air of easy access to the current top directors and CEOs in their communities. May they have every success in reaching out to those contacts.

But what about those not so well connected? What about the new person in town, or the young person on the rise, or the introvert? Do they have a chance at claiming a seat at the boardroom table? The answer is yes.

They just need to keep in mind our three key approaches:

▶ **Networking your connections with personal relationships.**
Start with and go deeper into your personal relationships.
They are your best natural source for the learning of, and
access to, boardroom connections.

▶ **Networking your connections with professional
relationships.** Strive to know and network with directors,
executives, and CEOs currently serving in boardrooms,
especially for those boards that interest you. And work
hard to *fish where the fish are.* As you think about this
tip to *fish where the fish are,* ask yourself and your
confidantes where you might naturally find an environment
that is known and comfortable for you, and gives
you the opportunity to interact with directors, executives,
and CEOs. For me, it was most always service on numerous
local nonprofit boards, fund-raising capital campaigns
(regularly led by community leaders and executives),
and local charity benefit balls. For my favorite certified
public accountant (CPA) in town, it is the annual
United Way campaign, the Mayor's annual prayer
breakfast that always turns out hundreds of directors
in one venue, and a rigorous golf schedule. For my
talented young life insurance agent on the rise, it is a
wide range of hunting and all things related to the local
Boy Scout events.

▶ **Your brand.** Constantly build your brand. Developing and
having some special set of skills, expertise, or character qualities that make you stand out from the crowd is vital and a sure
way to get noticed. Get noticed!

FIGURE 1.5 Sample Profile: Short and Sweet

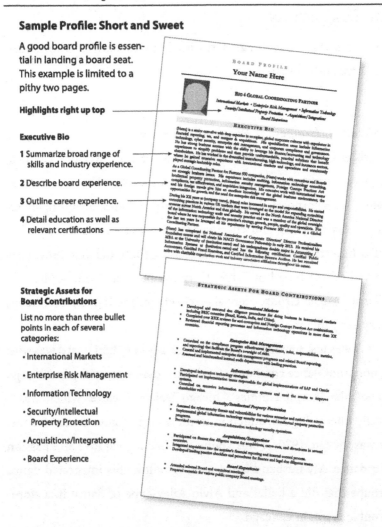

Sample Profile: Short and Sweet

A good board profile is essential in landing a board seat. This example is limited to a pithy two pages.

Highlights right up top

Executive Bio

1 Summarize broad range of skills and industry experience.

2 Describe board experience.

3 Outline career experience.

4 Detail education as well as relevant certifications

Strategic Assets for Board Contributions

List no more than three bullet points in each of several categories:

- International Markets
- Enterprise Risk Management
- Information Technology
- Security/Intellectual Property Protection
- Acquisitions/Integrations
- Board Experience

A good board profile is essential in landing a board seat. This example is limited to a pithy two pages.

The pursuit of a boardroom seat is similar to a job search, and almost all of us have first-hand experience with those. As in job searches, networking is often what works, but recruiters can be involved as well. See Figure 1.5 for a sample board profile.

Joining My First or Next Board of Directors

Here are three encouraging stories from executives who landed their first board seats.

Michele J. Hooper: A Passion for Dance

Michele J. Hooper is president and CEO of The Directors' Council, a private company that she cofounded in 2003. The organization works with corporate boards on a variety of issues, including diversity, independence, and effectiveness. Hooper sits on the board of PPG Industries, Inc. and UnitedHealth Group, Inc. She previously served on the board of Target Corporation, AstraZeneca plc., and Warner Music Group. Here she reflects on joining her first board very early in her career:

"I was just starting my work career. My very first board was with a nonprofit dance company—a modern dance company in Chicago called the Joseph Holmes Chicago Dance Theatre, which was a really interesting introduction to the world of governance for me. It was the late 1970s. I was young and had a great love and passion for dance. My husband and I used to follow this integrated dance troupe that did a ballet and Alvin Ailey–type of dance in a storefront location in Chicago.

"They charged next to nothing. You sat on folding chairs and there would be a handful of people in the audience that loved dance. We were part of the audience that knew they were fabulous.

"We had an extra hundred dollars that we decided we wanted to donate to this dance theater. I didn't know how to send it to them or what to spend it on so I called the dance studio and the phone was answered by Joseph [Holmes]. I told him, 'I have this extra hundred dollars, I'd love to donate it, and I love this group.' We talked and Joseph invited me to come learn more about the dance troupe at their board meeting.

"I go to this meeting which has a handful of people present, patrons who donated money and dancers. There was no agenda and the conversation wandered from topic to topic. So I start asking lots of routine business-type questions, and by the end of the meeting Joseph asks if I'd like to come on the board. I didn't know what their priorities were or where this was heading, (but) I said, 'Sure!'

"By the end of the next meeting I was offered chairman of the board. And I said, well, let me think about it. Let me look at the bylaws, surprisingly they did have bylaws—but the first thing their bylaws started out with was that you had to be a dancer to be on the board. Needless to say we spent time talking about the role of the board and fund raising and the value that could be brought to the company.

"And the dance company and its governance structure were built from there. They started out with six people dancing in a storefront in 1976, and by the time I left they grew from six dancers to 20 full-time dancers with the ability to have a salary, commissioned choreography, and music. They had the opportunity to dance on the stage at the Civic Opera and at the Auditorium Theatre. It was tremendous to see these gifted people who loved dance be able to have the funding and structure to move to the next level. Joseph Holmes Dance Theatre was my first board, and it was a really terrific learning experience serving with a great group of people in a field that I love."

Mellody Hobson Joins the Starbucks Corporation's Board at Age 36

Many of us are prone to think boards grow mostly out of the old school network and similar relationships. To be sure, for decades, male corporate executives have dominated most boards and when they went recruiting they tended to select people who were close to them and more usually thought like them. But that is changing. Increasingly, board recruiters look for people with diverse skills, background, and experience. Gender and skin color take a back seat or are regarded as a plus because growing up female or as a person of color provides a different and valued perspective.

Mellody Hobson of Ariel Investments, LLC (formerly Ariel Capital Management) noted that sometimes women are reluctant to take on a role outside their companies. "With some women, even in my own firm, you have to sort of push them out because they think, 'I've got to do a really good job, which means staying very focused,'" she told the *Wall Street Journal* in an interview that was featured in the *Journal* in April 2011.[8] But "I learned very early that I can do a better job if I have other stimuli that give me a broader perspective. And what people with that focused mind-set don't realize is how important those outside relationships can be."

The way in which Hobson landed her board seat is instructive. She got out of the office. "I helped Bill Bradley when he ran for president in 2000," Hobson recalled. "I worked as hard on his campaign as I worked on my job every single day. Obviously, we were unsuccessful. But then one day, Bill calls and says, 'I'm on the board of Starbucks, and I'm taking you with me.' . . . . I never imagined that was possible. I'm like this pipsqueak in Chicago."

Hobson was, of course, being enormously modest. By 2000, she had risen to be president of Ariel, a firm that manages over $3 billion in assets. She had, however, been a pipsqueak of sorts. After graduating from Princeton, Hobson started at Ariel as an intern. Then she rose to the top and made it on to a prestigious board in ways that we can all learn from. One way is to peer beyond the horizon and recognize that your skills and attributes can be valuable to others. By forging those connections, you can also help the company that gave you your start.

Hobson essentially made a name for herself with the Bradley campaign. She got noticed and, voila, Bill Bradley introduces her to the people at Starbucks. You, too, can plant the "I'm-taking-you-with-me" notion in the heads of people who sit on boards that interest you.

James Turley Finds the Right Fit

James S. Turley did not have to go looking for board opportunities. He had the pedigree and brand to attract lots of offers. Turley is the retired chairman and CEO of Ernst & Young, one of the largest professional services organizations in the world. Not long after leaving that job, Turley was elected to board seats at St. Louis–based Emerson, a global manufacturing and technology concern, and Citigroup, a leading global bank.

With Turley's superb track record as a leader, his background in finance, accounting, and with connections all over the globe, he could pretty much write his own ticket as far as a board seat was concerned. Perhaps few of you reading this are so well positioned, but we include Turley here because of his insights in thinking about a board position and also as someone who has done his share of recruiting.

The first thing that may strike you about Turley is that he sounds genuinely down to earth, even humble. He says he didn't want to take on a board position unless he could have time to fully participate. So if the schedules don't mesh, the position offered would be a nonstarter, and, he says, there's a lot of homework to be done. Not just reading, but sitting down with managers and understanding how they see the business and how they think. "These are serious roles," he said. "You don't just get to hang out."

"If something seems wrong, it's your job to raise your hand and ask for clarification."

The best way to think about your job is as one who is empowered to ask any question as a director. You are not management. Your job is to provide governance and oversight. A lot of directors ask very good questions not just of management, but of each other. And they listen intently to the answers.

As far as recruiting is concerned, Turley said when he was helping to build Ernst & Young he sought "different perspectives." "The last thing you want is everyone who looks alike, talks alike, and went to the same schools. . . . We think about what skills we need added to this board, international experience, data experience, and audit experience."

Like many, Turley said you are unlikely to get a board seat by sending in an application and letting people know you are smart. "You just let people know, this is something I'd like. This is the type of company I think I could add value to, and please keep me in mind. I have had people have that discussion with me." And when the opportunity arose, Turley said, he would play the role of an informal matchmaker.

And it has to be a good fit. "The important thing is to think through how you feel about management and your fellow board members. What about the industry sector? Is this sector interesting to you? Is there somewhere that I can add value? Is it something where I can learn something, too? If you are continuing to learn you will be more into it, too."

DIRECTOR SEARCHES FROM A SKILLS-DRIVEN PROCESS

Now let's look at another path to a board seat. Many director searches today start through a skills-driven process.

In preparation for director searches, boards perform an inventory and analysis of the skills, expertise, and talents they have with their current directors. The board then asks what skills does the board need going forward for some relevant time frame to best meet the needs of the company. For example, you might have a company that has plans to expand for the first time into trade in South America, and the current directors have no experience with this type of trade or in doing business in South America.

Another example would be two recent director searches by a large U.S.–based privately owned stock market brokerage firm. The firm had experienced rapid growth and decided to add both a commercial bank and a trust company to complement the services the brokerage firm offered. The board initially sought two new directors with deep experience in commercial banking and years of experience owning and operating a large trust company. Given the level of deep financial knowledge involved with running both a commercial bank and a trust company, and the rapid growth that the new bank and trust company experienced, the brokerage firm quickly opted to seek a third new director. That individual brought deep financial reporting and auditing experience.

It is important to note that this skills-driven process falls into the broader topic of overall board composition. Board composition focuses on answering the question: "All things considered how does a company bring together the right group of people?"

Skills can be focused on technical aptitude. But they can also include ideal personal attributes, or a broader range of other factors like representing a particular geographic location or unique market or adding diversity.

Here's an example of a skills and competency checklist for a recent new director search based on a regional retailer that markets to young consumers:

Skills Sought:
- ► Known in our fashion industry
- ► Respected executive experience
- ► Sales and marketing history in particular
- ► Deep knowledge of current trends in selling to youth

Personal Attributes:
- ► Impeccable reputation for integrity
- ► Understands familyowned business
- ► Able to work with a group, yet independent-minded

Unique Talents:

► Gets our "Southern" ways

► Knows our special "Southern" customers

► Especially knows "Midwestern" customers we
aim to have

Similarly, here's a checklist for a large Midwest private
mining company, seeking a director from outside the family.

Our Top Priorities:

► Prior board experience

► Corporate finance experience

► Senior business management experience

► Exposure to the family business environment

Strong Preference for:

► A Southern Illinois location

► Top analytical competence (qualitative and
quantitative)

► Familiarity with natural resource or asset-based
enterprises

It Is Important That the Director Be:

► Collegial with collaborative approach

► Independent in thought and judgment

Additional Desirable Experience:

► Real estate development experience

► Business policy and planning (strategic and
business plans)

(Continued)

Other Highly Desirable Qualities:
- ► Creative and innovative thinker
- ► Tolerance and patience with family dimension
- ► Congenial personality and good chemistry with board
- ► Demonstrated commitment to organization and goals

UnitedHealth Group, a public company, has developed a highly refined skills matrix. The matrix accounts for the company's near and long-term strategies and how new members "would complement or enhance the skills represented by the current Board members."

UnitedHealth divides the matrix into two sections: "a list of core criteria that every member of the Board should meet and a list of skills and attributes desired to be represented on the Board as a whole, with a goal of having members of the Board possess one or more of the collective skills and attributes listed."

Included on the core criteria list:

- ► High integrity and ethical standards
- ► Standing and reputation in the individual's field
- ► Risk oversight ability, with respect to the particular skills of the individual director that are reflected in the collective skills section of the skills matrix
- ► Understanding of and experience with complex public companies or like organizations

► Ability to work collegially and collaboratively with other directors and management

Included among the skills desired on the board as a whole:

► Corporate governance expertise
► Financial expertise
► Health care industry expertise
► Direct consumer marketing expertise
► Brand marketing/public relations expertise
► Diversity
► Legal expertise
► Capital markets expertise
► Political/health care policy expertise
► Clinical practice
► Technology/business process expertise

Industry Surveys List Key Board Attributes

Industry surveys also shed light on what companies have on their wish lists for new board members. A leading executive search firm, Spencer Stuart, conducts annual public company board surveys and publishes the *Spencer Stuart Board Index (SSBI)*. See Figure 1.6 for a chart of key attributes sought.

These examples provide evidence that director searches today do often start with a skills-driven process. Accordingly, if you are serious about claiming a seat in a boardroom, begin developing a powerful and current resume that clearly identifies your strongest skills and expertise.

Figure 1.6 What Are They Looking For?

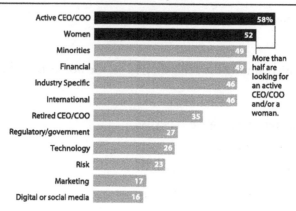

Industry surveys shed light on what companies are looking for in new board members. A leading executive search firm, Spencer Stuart, has conducted an annual public company board survey for many years and publishes the *Spencer Stuart Board Index (SSBI)*. Their 2012 survey of 87 respondents reflected the following Wish List for New Director Backgrounds or Expertise.

Source: Spencer Stuart Board Index, 2012.

Now let's focus on how you might go about researching your first board opportunity.

RESEARCH

There are a handful of standard approaches to research that have proven effective over the years in identifying boardroom opportunities. These include:

▶ Do your own research on organizations and associations that are part of the governance world and join those where they have an active approach to identifying and circulating boardroom opportunities. Recommended resources include director directories or registries, such as that of the National Association of Corporate Directors (NACD), which allows members to create a profile and be contacted by interested companies and uses its registry to recommend individuals to companies looking for credentialed and prepared board members. Other groups with registries or directories include the International Women's Forum (IWF), the nonprofit organization Catalyst, the American Institute of Certified Public Accountants (AICPA), and the Institute of Corporate Directors (ICD).

▶ Find the major search firm websites that provide information on board opportunities, including Spencer Stuart, Heidrick & Struggles, Russell Reynolds Associates, Egon Zehnder, and more.

▶ Plug into and learn the governance world by attending conferences and reaching out to the people you know on boards and who are active in the governance world.

▶ Pursue advertisements for board opportunities. They do not come around often. Advertising for directors is far from becoming a trend, but opportunities really do show up.

▶ Watch closely to spot opportunities that might arise with companies you have an interest in by following their life cycles and activities.

That last item brings us to my client Jane and how she landed her first board seat. Jane had closely followed the travails of a publicly traded company in higher education, her field of expertise.

Her legal and regulatory experience clued her into some major changes that were likely coming to the company. As Jane foresaw, the company soon hired a new CEO and announced that two new directors would be added, with a local search firm handling the searches.

Jane knew from her research the two firms that would likely handle this specialized search and quickly learned the names of the lead partners who would be involved. Then, via express mail, she sent a carefully crafted letter of personal introduction to the partners advising that it was time in her career to pursue a board opportunity. She highlighted her deep regulatory experience in higher education, and shined a light on a number of her talents.

Jane received a form letter of thanks immediately from one firm and the promise to add her to their general director database, and that was the last she heard from them. Two days later, Jane received a phone call from a junior search associate with the other search firm. She made it through a phone interview and into an airport interview with the search team, and was ultimately put on the short list of board candidates. She was not selected to join this board. A person recently retired with years of experience in the U.S. Department of Education, who Jane knew well from her own industry contacts, was picked and offered the boardroom seat. Still, Jane gained valuable experience, great connections, and motivation to do more research on great opportunities.

Believe It or Not!

Board opportunities can show up in the most unusual places if you watch for them.

In the believe it or not category, legendary investor Warren Buffett of Berkshire Hathaway fame went public a few years back with his quest to add four new directors to serve on his board for the long term. Twenty persons responded to his public request and several were seriously considered. A deep knowledge of operating businesses and investment management were key requirements. One of the unspoken requirements was a substantial investment in Berkshire Hathaway stock. Ultimately, Berkshire Hathaway added four new directors that each held millions in Berkshire Hathaway stock.

Let's look at two other cases of how others used research to find their first boardroom seat.

John

John lives in a medically underserved area on the edge of a major metropolitan town. He has a great career that he loves in a low-paying field, and has always considered himself a consumer advocate, with a special interest in the health care field. John learned from research that the large health center his family uses is part of a special Health Resources Service Administration Health Center program operated by the U.S. Department of Health and Human Services. It is

(Continued)

community-based and patient-directed and specially designed for communities with limited access to health care.

A special mandate of the Health Center program is governance by and for the people served. At least 51 percent of the board's members must be patients or consumers of the health center. Having this information on board member requirements, and having a lot of talent to offer, John was able within a year's time to position himself with the health center leadership and board for election. It turns out they had a special need just at that time to add board members that qualified as patients or consumers, and John had a number of community leadership qualities that were needed as well.

Now John is on a fast track for leadership of the full board, having been elected a key officer of the board in just a few short years. Most interesting, two other board opportunities are now on John's radar, one volunteer and one paid, based on relationships he developed in the health center board room.

Maggie Wilderotter

At the 2013 annual conference of the National Association of Corporate Directors, Maggie Wilderotter, CEO of the public company Frontier Communications, shared this story:

"I was 28 and vice president of sales at a small vendor to cable companies when I decided to try to get elected to the board of the National Cable & Telecommunications Association (NCTA). I called all 2,000 industry vendors and promised to represent them if they sent in proxy votes for me. I won on my second try in 1987.

"There was only one other female director, and I was at least three management levels below everyone else. But I became very active. I wrote a newsletter, and I befriended all the CEOs. Not only did this help me get more business for my company, but I got to know people who recommended me to join the company boards they served on. I even got my CEO job through my board connections. I'd already served on a board with many of the directors who recruited me to be a CEO."[9]

Obviously, her early skills of spotting opportunities and networking extensively added to her long-term career success along with many new board opportunities. And may I say thanks to her for sharing her experience and introducing me to the very important term of *fish where the fish are.*

Where will you start fishing for your first or next boardroom seat?

Chapter 2

BEING AN EFFECTIVE DIRECTOR

Every director owes a duty of care and loyalty in serving on a board. Every director individually, and the board acting in concert, has a fiduciary duty to act in the best interest of the corporation and its stockholders overall.

So let's ask three basic questions:

- ► Who owns and controls a corporation?
- ► What is a fiduciary and a fiduciary duty?
- ► What about all the Delaware corporations?

WHO OWNS AND CONTROLS A CORPORATION?

All states have state-enacted laws built on a corporate model that separates ownership from control. The owners of a corporation are its shareholders and the shareholders, operating under state laws where they are incorporated, are charged with electing and removing directors. This board of directors is thereby responsible for taking charge and control of the operations and assets of the corporation on behalf of the shareholders. It is common practice for the board of directors of a corporation to delegate the daily business operations to one or more executives routinely known as the "management."

The shareholders elect the directors. The directors appoint the executive officers. The directors are responsible to the shareholders and the executive officers are responsible to the board of directors. Of note, courts regularly find that executive officers have a joint responsibility and accountability to both the board of directors and shareholders of a corporation.[1]

At the basic level, shareholders own, directors control, and management runs a corporation.

What is a Fiduciary and a Fiduciary Duty?

A *fiduciary* is a person to whom property or power is entrusted for the benefit of another.[2] Fiduciaries are vested with special privileges and responsibilities while acting for the benefit of others. Think of a trustee who is appointed as guardian for the benefit and care of a minor child. Think of an executor or personal representative who is appointed to handle the estate of a deceased person. And think of directors who are responsible for taking charge and control of the operations and assets of the corporation on behalf of the shareholders.

Courts analyzing the duties owed by directors have found that it is incorrect to say that the fiduciary duty of a corporate director is the same as that of a trustee of a trust,[3] because "[t]he classic trusteeship is not essentially a risk-taking enterprise, but a caretaking one," while diligent directors necessarily must make decisions that carry some risk. Trust law also carries an absolute prohibition on self-dealing, while corporate law has relaxed the requirements of directors to avoid self-dealing, albeit only if the corporation is unharmed.

The confusion with trust law is exacerbated in situations where directors are called "trustees," such as at some nonprofits and charities. There, the term "trustees" is used not to invoke trust law protections or duties, but instead in order to imply the custodial function that comes along with being on the board of a social benefit entity.

In general, a *fiduciary duty* pertains to the relationship and obligation between fiduciaries and the people they serve and to whom their obligation is owed. Directors and boards of directors are fiduciaries. The directors by virtue of their legitimate election are vested with special privileges and responsibilities while acting for the benefit of others.

Being a fiduciary and having a fiduciary duty implies a position of great trust, requiring any number of qualities and duties including good faith, trustworthiness, and confidence. It requires a very high level of care in managing the assets, money, and operations of another.[4]

Two fiduciary duties of directors are widely recognized:

- ▸ The duty of care
- ▸ The duty of loyalty

The duties of care and loyalty are considered creations of the common law of various states and subject to ongoing reviews and interpretations by the courts.

Using the simplest of definitions, the *duty of care* means that directors be careful, informed, and use their own independent judgment. The *duty of loyalty* means that directors use their authority only in the best interest of the corporation and never only in their own personal interest or the interest of some other party.

Other fiduciary duties surface from time to time, often when novel legal claims against directors are being put forth. These include the duties of good faith, fair dealing, candor, confidentiality, full disclosure, and more.[5]

What About All of Those Delaware Corporations?

In the United States, a corporation comes into being under the authority of a state of incorporation, with the choice of the state being made by those persons filing the application for incorporation. The general corporate laws for a state of incorporation—along with shareholder-approved governing documents including articles of incorporation and bylaws—establish the general contract, obligations, and relationships among the shareholders, directors, and other parties to company operations.

For those knowledgeable in the world of corporate law, the state of Delaware and its specialized business-oriented court system are preeminent thought leaders in corporate and fiduciary duty law. Many states look to Delaware law to guide them in developing and applying laws that govern non-Delaware corporations. The importance of Delaware law is especially notable for large publicly traded companies as more than 50 percent of all publicly traded U.S. corporations and more than 60 percent of the Fortune 500 companies are incorporated in Delaware.[6] Delaware clearly has a prosperous business, with its renowned court system that is well supported by its state legislature. The law in all 50 states tells us that the board oversees a company's operations with language similar to that found in the General Corporation Law of Delaware shown in Figure 2.1 from Title 8, Chapter 1, Subsection 141 on Directors and Officers.

FIGURE 2.1 Title 8 Corporations Law

TITLE 8

Corporations

CHAPTER 1. GENERAL CORPORATION LAW

Subchapter IV. Directors and Officers

§ 141 Board of directors; powers; number, qualifications, terms and quorum; committees; classes of directors; nonstock corporations; reliance upon books; action without meeting; removal.

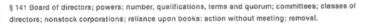

(a) The business and affairs of every corporation organized under this chapter shall be managed by or under the direction of a board of directors, except as may be otherwise provided in this chapter or in its certificate of incorporation. If any such provision is made in the certificate of incorporation, the powers and duties conferred or imposed upon the board of directors by this chapter shall be exercised or performed to such extent and by such person or persons as shall be provided in the certificate of incorporation.

The fundamental role of the board is to oversee or direct management by monitoring performance and compliance with policies and law. It is important to note that these are delegated duties. If there is no management, or a controlling or dominant shareholder that decides to manage directly as with some privately held companies, the board may in fact manage. Likewise, if there is some important area that is not being properly handled by management, the board can at times step in to fulfill the role of management. There are three notable examples of boards stepping into a management role:

1. The first example is a company that suddenly loses the services of a CEO for some reason such as illness, death, or termination, and a current board member steps in on an interim basis.

2. The second example is somewhat similar to the first. Many nonprofits over the years have been stretched for talent and staff. As a consequence, it is common to find board members

performing any number of executive and staff functions for the nonprofit.

3. The third example has board members acting as managers for start-up companies in the early stages of operation.

Don't Be Sleazy, Sloppy, or Naïve

Don't be sleazy. Don't be sloppy. Don't be naïve. Know the "Business Judgment Rule."

We have seen that a director's basic duties overall begin and end with the law and basic legal obligations. No surprise there. And for all the complexity in the law, the good news is that directors can enter the boardroom with great confidence if they can grasp the two basic duties that establish the standards of conduct: a duty of care and a duty of loyalty. Let's look at simple definitions for the duty of care and the duty of loyalty.

Reviewing, the *duty of care* means that directors be informed, diligent, and use their own independent judgment. The *duty of loyalty* means that directors use their authority only in the best interest of the corporation and never only in their own personal interest or the interest of some other party. It is that simple.

For most prospective directors, director liability is the one question and concern that inevitably surfaces and often causes anxiety. The best answer and protection any director can rely upon in fulfilling his or her duties is a simple concept known as the Business Judgment Rule.

The Business Judgment Rule provides directors with a shield of liability protection. It is a principle well established in case law that courts follow where they decline to substitute their judgment for that of directors and management. If the actions of a board of directors produce a bad result, even a mind-boggling string of bad results, courts consistently decline to second-guess directors. This is why we see major corporations, such as Hewlett-Packard (HP) and The Walt Disney Company (Disney), winning cases in which their boards have been accused of failing to do their duties. Examples include a suit in which HP directors were accused of failing to properly oversee CEO succession and acquisitions, and Disney directors allegedly squandering some $140 million with a severance package given to executive Michael Ovitz after just a year of service.

When the duty of care and the duty of loyalty are understood and well applied by a director, these two duties in concert with the Business Judgment Rule provide broad protections from director liability. Is it really that simple to perform a director's basic duty without great risk of director liability? Yes, but that is where the offhand and slang expression "don't be sloppy and don't be sleazy" speaks volumes to directors.

Don't be sloppy. Though Disney prevailed in the Ovitz case, its directors paid a high price with years of public and expensive litigation.

Don't be sleazy. Sometimes companies hide their dirty laundry in an attempt to appear upright to the rest of the world. In February 2011, Englishman Michael Woodford became president of Japanese-based multinational giant Olympus, and discovered 20 years of deception and fraud valued at some $1.7 billion in hidden losses.[7] Woodford took the information into the boardroom. Instead of working to solve the problem, the board of directors fired Woodford, who then returned to England and blew the whistle.

The greatest real risk of liability for any director is reputational risk for the corporation and its directors. Don't be sleazy and don't be sloppy is a sure home remedy against liability.

Don't be naïve. The duty of care expects a director to be reasonably well informed, to actively participate in decision making, and to perform all acts with the care of an ordinarily prudent person in similar circumstances. In practice this means you show up for meetings. You exercise your own independent judgment in making corporate decisions, and you work to be reasonably well informed. You may rely on information supplied by staff and advisors. You may delegate much of the work to the corporation staff, given that directors do not operate the day-to-day business. Even so, your basic director responsibilities may not be delegated.

You dig deeper through and with management on matters that are unclear. You ask for experts to review matters that are important enough to require technical expertise. You strive to maintain a strong healthy relationship with management, but you never hesitate to maintain a healthy skepticism in your role as a director.

The duty of loyalty expects that directors will never use their board position to gain a personal advantage to the detriment of the corporation. In practice this means no conflicts of interest. You should not take personal advantage of any opportunities that rightfully belong to the corporation first, and you should keep corporate business matters confidential until they are public record.

The Business Judgment Rule provides comfort and protection for directors. All the real benefits of the Business Judgment Rule can be lost in situations where there is intentional bad behavior on the part of the director. Examples of such bad behavior include criminal activity, fraud, bad faith, gross negligence of your duties as a director, and willful bad acts.

Remember the Disney-Ovitz case? The court's scathing review included strong indications that while the matter at hand passed a *minimum acceptable standard* at the time, Disney and others must have every expectation that their actions were unlikely to meet current standards. Don't be naïve and don't expect the Business Judgment Rule to protect every action or challenge.

Beyond knowing the duty of care, the duty of loyalty, and the Business Judgment Rule, there are two other concepts to consider:

▶ Independence and Independent-Minded
▶ Conflicts of Interest and Related Party Transactions

INDEPENDENCE AND INDEPENDENT-MINDED

The word *independence* carries a special meaning, and has a variety of interpretations, in the boardroom. In this setting, there is little unanimity concerning its value.

In the boardroom, it is vitally important to have a good grasp and understanding of the word *independence,* the term *to be independent-minded*, and the overall topic of director independence and independent directors. These concepts are vital to a robust understanding of governance and how boards work today.

First, let's review a bit of history concerning how independence came to be applied to corporate governance. From the earliest days of common and corporate law in America, directors of corporations were expected to make every effort to avoid being involved in company decisions and transactions where they had a personal stake that might conflict with the interests of the companies they serve. The director owed his loyalty first to the company.

This concept was enshrined to a great degree in the Securities Act of 1933, which followed the Stock Market Crash of 1929. The act created the Securities and Exchange Commission (SEC). The SEC regulated the sale of securities and was given the general mandate of protecting investors.[8] One way to do that was to promote sound corporate governance practices, which the SEC has steadily pursued at a snail's pace over the ensuing decades.

A string of financial crises, bubbles, and business scandals from 2000 through 2008 set the stage for the SEC to more formally establish its views regarding the importance of independence and independent directors particularly in the running of public company boards. The Sarbanes-Oxley Act (SOX) of 2002 and the Dodd-Frank Wall Street Reform and Consumer Protection Act of 2010 (Dodd-Frank Act) set forth rules for the SEC to use in specific circumstances.

A clear theme that has emerged from the SEC is the view that independent directors ought to have increasing control of public company boardrooms, rather than inside directors commonly known as management. Publicly listed companies today are required by various SEC rules to have only independent directors serving on the key board committees known as nominating and governance, compensation and audit.

That all sounds prudent and straightforward. But the concept of independence is also fraught with nuances and complexity. Independent directors are now meeting a rising tide of expectations that has greatly increased their workloads and sometimes puts them in peril. Typical public company directors have, in the last decade, seen their time spent on board duties increase from 100 or so hours per year to 250 hours or more.[9]

Even that might not be enough. Independent directors face the challenge of staying fully informed about the company they serve—given limited time, unlimited complexity, and an endless supply of information. When considering the time demands of directors staying fully informed in an era of ever-increasing regulation, I am reminded of a governance story from a favorite unnamed executive on the topic of time demands. It seems he was meeting with the key staff of several agencies that influence legislation impacting governance. In general conversation on several new bills, the staffers were shocked to learn that the board directors did not work full time for their boards, especially given the compensation levels.

Directors typically meet only six to eight times per year. The company in general, and management in particular, typically has more information than can be taken in by any one director. Often, independent directors have backgrounds and knowledge different from the specific industry of the board they serve. Conversely, inside directors, made up of active or retired managers, almost always have in-depth hands-on knowledge concerning the company and the industry within which it operates.

While I personally subscribe to the great value that independent directors can bring to most any board, many others do not take that as a given. Professor Jeffrey A. Sonnenfeld is one of the contrarians. In his classic must read *Harvard Business Review* article "What Makes Great Boards Great" article, he notes that when he compares samples of the least- and most-admired companies listed in *Fortune* magazine, there is no meaningful distinction related to independence.[10] He makes the observation that inside directors are often far more plugged in, willing and able to debate the CEO on important matters than independent directors. Personally, I am not so sure. While I have seen great boards where the senior executives serving as inside directors were welcome to vigorously share their thoughts with the board and even debate the CEO and other directors, I have seen far more boardrooms where there was a remarkable degree of silence from inside directors in the presence of the CEO.

Along the same lines, we can find many notable companies with robust commitments to independence and independent directors that have experienced major company and governance-related failures. To wit: Enron, WorldCom, HealthSouth, and Tyco.

Legendary investor Warren Buffett has years of success with business, investing, and the related topic of governance. So his views are worth taking into account. His observations on governance have been weaved into his annual letters to Berkshire Hathaway shareholders for decades. They are pithy, laced with humor, and well thought out. Importantly, they come from serving in 19 boardrooms, knowing hundreds of directors, and being challenged by others regarding his director independence on the Coca-Cola board and others.

In his 1993 annual letter, Buffett stated that directors have to get rid of a manager who is mediocre or worse, no matter how likeable. Likewise, he said if greedy managers overreach and dip too deeply into the shareholders' pockets, directors must slap their hands. Here he is speaking of unreasonable executive compensation along with unwise acquisitions or the waste of company assets. This is from a man known to pay well for top executive performance.[11]

Buffett decries a "boardroom atmosphere" that makes it socially awkward to question management. Likewise, he believes soaring public company director fees add to the problem. He says, ". . . a director whose moderate income is heavily dependent on directors' fees—and who hopes mightily to be invited to join other boards in order to earn more fees—is highly unlikely to offend a CEO or fellow directors, who in a major way will determine his reputation in corporate circles."[12]

Buffett's long-standing suggested criteria for great directors are that they be "owner-oriented, business-savvy, interested, and truly independent."[13] The best summary I can give of Buffett's thinking on good governance and independence is to provide his thoughts from the time when he was challenged on his own independence while serving on the board of Coca-Cola. Critics said Buffett lacked "independence" because some of the companies he owned provided routine services to Coca-Cola. One group wanted him removed from the board and another wanted him removed from the audit committee.[14]

Said Buffett:

I can't resist mentioning that Jesus understood the calibration of independence far more clearly than do the protesting institutions. In Matthew 6:21, he observed: "For where your treasure is, there will your heart be also." Even to an institutional investor, $8 billion should qualify as "treasure" that dwarfs any profits Berkshire might earn on its routine transactions with Coke.

Measured by the biblical standard, the Berkshire board itself is a model: (a) *every* director is a member of a family owning at least $4 million of stock; (b) *none* of these shares were acquired from Berkshire via options or grants; (c) *no* directors receive committee, consulting, or board fees from the company that are more than a tiny portion of their annual incomes; and (d) although we have a standard indemnity arrangement, we carry no liability insurance for directors.

At Berkshire, board members travel the same road as shareholders.[15]

What Does It Really Mean to be Independent-Minded?

Ultimately, independence in any environment means the trait and ability to be independent-minded—to be free from any strings that might be attached to a particular decision or transaction. It means to have no direct or indirect material personal interest in a decision or transaction in any way, shape, or form. It also means, at critical times, the courage and ability to speak the truth in difficult circumstances, and to challenge the status quo or conventional wisdom.

It means the ability and moral courage to be able to stand alone, because it is the right thing to do, even if it costs you something in any number of ways such as financially, socially, politically, or your good reputation. Indeed, having the ability and moral courage to stand alone can at times even cost you your seat on the board of directors, or prevent you from gaining a future board seat. Be prudent, be judicious, and speak the truth as required. It pays in the long run.

I mentioned that I personally believe in the great value that independent directors can bring to most any board. In part that belief stems from several postbubble reforms that have strengthened the hand of independent directors, especially with public company boards.

The first reform involves regular boardroom executive sessions, which are gaining wide acceptance. *Executive sessions* are meetings of independent directors without the CEO or management present. This reduces the social risk of speaking out against a powerful executive or a dubious idea. Major stock exchange listing requirements for the New York Stock Exchange (NYSE) and the NASDAQ (National Association of Securities Dealers Automated Quotes) now effectively require their member boards to hold executive sessions without the CEO or management involved.

The second reform is a major shift away from the leadership of one person holding the combined CEO and board chair role. Again, public companies are leading the change in response to listing requirements. In a 2013 report only 19 percent of new CEOs were given the combined role of board chair as well.[16] A top 2012 report shows that over 90 percent of Standard & Poor's (S&P) company boards have an independent board chair, lead director, or presiding director.[17] Curiously, the vast majority of these boards have not made formal changes to their bylaws and related corporate documents requiring these changes, but have used informal actions perhaps to maintain their options long term.

The third reform is the change to the independent auditor relationship. Previously external independent auditors effectively reported to management. Today boards hire the independent auditors, who are accountable to them. At public companies, board audit committees are made up exclusively of independent directors.[18]

The fourth reform is the requirement for public companies to have authentic whistleblower hotlines. In the past, such hotlines, where they existed, often rang on the desk of a company employee. In some cases it was the desk of the CEO's secretary or a company lawyer. Today, the requirement is that hotline systems for the reporting, receipt, and investigation of concerns about alleged legal or ethical violations in the company channel through the audit committee and its independent directors.[19] Alternately, and much to the dismay of the many in the corporate world, the SEC has also developed an incentive reward system where whistleblowers can in many circumstances elect to proceed through the SEC.

I have had the personal benefit of seeing independent-minded directors speak the truth in the boardroom when faced with difficult circumstances, so I know it can be done, even without the benefit of executive sessions. Fortunately for me, in most of the cases I witnessed, the truth was spoken in an agreeable, firm, and direct way.

A final caution on the use and meaning of independence. As you fulfill your duties as an independent-minded board member, you might run into several other terms that use or relate to the word *independence* in describing related business operations. Here are a few of the key terms that touch on independence:

Outside Director: A director not employed by the company and independent director.

Inside Director: A director also employed by the company and nonindependent director.

Management Director: A director also employed in management.

Nonmanagement Director: A director not employed in the management.

Nonmanagement Insider: A director who previously worked for the company.

Insider: This relates specifically to securities law requirements for the proper disclosure by any person in a company, director or not, buying or selling stock.

Independent Chairman: An independent director, not employed by the company, serving as chairman of the board of directors of the company.

Independent Auditor: A certified public accountant, who examines the financial records and business transactions of a company that he or she is not affiliated with. An independent auditor is typically used to avoid conflicts of interest and to ensure the integrity of the auditing process. Independent auditors are sometimes called external auditors.[20]

Be on the alert when the terms *independent, independence,* or *independent-minded* surface. Never be shy about clarifying or confirming the definition of these important terms with your fellow board members, management, or legal counsel. Above all, never be shy about speaking the truth in the boardroom when that is called for. You will be glad you did and be properly fulfilling your duties as a director.

CONFLICTS OF INTEREST AND RELATED-PARTY TRANSACTIONS

The duty of loyalty requires directors to exercise their powers in the interest of the company and not in their own interest or the interest of another entity or person. Directors as fiduciaries have a duty of undivided loyalty to the company they serve, which includes reasonable expectations of restrictions against competing against the company.

Reasonable restrictions against competing would include the following examples:

- ▶ Not seeking to actively compete with the company
- ▶ Not pursuing company business or personnel
- ▶ Not having large ownership in entities that compete with the company
- ▶ Not receiving secret commissions on company transactions
- ▶ Not disclosing company trade secrets or confidential information to others or using for personal gain

Having a Conflicting Interest

Directors may at times have interests in conflict with those of the company. The duty of loyalty requires that a director be conscious of the potential for such conflicts and act with candor and care in dealing with such situations.

Conflicts of interest involving a director are not inherently illegal; nor are they to be regarded as a negative reflection on the integrity of the board or the director. It is the manner in which the director and the board deal with a disclosed conflict that determines the propriety of the transaction.

A director should be sensitive to any interest he or she may have in a decision to be made by the board of directors and, as far as possible, recognize and disclose such interest prior to it coming to the attention of, or before, the board.

To properly address potential conflicts of interest with the board, the first rule is awareness, the second rule is disclosure, and the third rule is disinterested review.

Seizing a Company Opportunity

Before a director engages in a transaction which he or she should reasonably know may be of interest to the company, the director should disclose the transaction to the company. The disclosure should provide sufficient detail and adequate time to enable the company to act or decline to act with regard to the transaction.

A corporate opportunity arises when a director knows that he or she can participate in a transaction which could plausibly fall within the company's present or future interests or activities. Good practice dictates the director present such opportunities to the board for review before participating in a transaction apart from the company.

Tools to Help Identify and Understand Potential Conflicts of Interest

A comprehensive list of the major ownership interests of a company, its subsidiary companies, and related interests ideally can be made available to help directors identify any potential conflicts of interest. Prospective and new directors can use a company-provided Conflict of Interest Disclosure Form to provide an initial comprehensive list of activities, affiliations, and major assets owned in the business markets and geographical locations where the company conducts its core businesses. This form can be updated annually.

Figure 2.2 features a table for boards to consider that reflects four possible standards to apply when considering conflicts of interest, including: No Standards, Standards Reflecting Minimum Legal Requirements, Standards Reflecting Principles of Good Governance, and Highest Possible Ethical Standards:

FIGURE 2.2 Possible Standards to Apply When Considering Conflicts of Interest

No Standards*　→　Highest standards

	No Standards*	Standards reflecting Minimum Legal Requirements	Standards Reflecting Principles of Good Governance	Highest Possible Ethical Standards
Board Focus	Directors avoid or ignore the issue of conflicts.	Directors follow the form and letter of the law related to conflicts.	Directors adhere to the substance and intent of the law related to conflicts.	Directors' actions reflect integrity beyond reproach.
Board Practice	Directors react to conflicts only when they surface as real "problems."	Directors attend to the basic legal formalities that are required to keep them safe.	Directors establish "Best Practices" to surface conflicts and provide independent review.	Directors assiduously seek to avoid conflicts, making this an organizational party.
Criteria for Determining Conflicts	Conflicts are recognized only after the application of some internal or external influence or force.	Conflicts are defined according to all applicable legal standards, including local rules, state statutes, federal laws (IRS, etc.), corporate articles and bylaws, company policies and procedures, attorney opinions and advice, and insurance contracts and policies.	All minimum legal requirements are applied. Board of the organization defines conflicts and encourages consistent compliance and disclosure: awareness is key applied through compliance work; disclosure is key and not discretionary; independent review is key to compliance.	Directors take the position that conflicts must be avoided and will not be permitted, except by rare exception.
Observed Frequency	Conflicts can occur without review.	Conflicts occasionally occur, usually with review.	Conflicts seldom occur, always with review.	Conflicts rarely occur, and only after independent review by exception.
Routine Policy	Conflicts policy does not exist or is not applied.	Conflicts policy exists, but policy may not be actively enforced.	Conflicts policy is regularly enforced, reviewed, and disclosed. The policy includes procedures for addressing conflicts.	The board builds on good governance by paying assiduous attention to conflicts, proactively developing ways to prevent or resolve them.

* Including vague or no standards.

Source: Tom Bakewell, "Handling Conflicts of Interest at the Board Level," *NACD Directors Monthly,* February 2001

Related-Party Transactions

A *related-party transaction* is a "business deal or arrangement between two parties who are joined by a special relationship prior to the deal."[21] Most related-party transactions do not lead to problems and are perfectly acceptable, but because of the special relationship there is a tendency to scrutinize them and keep an eye out for conflict of interest.

American public companies are required to disclose such transactions. The disclosure should include:

▶ A discussion of the nature of the relationship of the people and/or entities involved
▶ A description of the transaction
▶ The amount of money or property at stake.

Examples of related parties include:

▶ Affiliates
▶ Principal owners
▶ Management
▶ Family members
▶ Voting stockholders

Some related-party transactions become problems and lead to SEC investigations. Most commonly are those involving loans to related parties and payments to company officers for either unapproved or nonexistent services.

The most notable incident regarding related-party transactions came with the Enron scandal. Enron's accounting for its "special-purpose entities (SPEs)" (the related parties) and sales of its own stock and assets to the SPEs, among other things, created a substantial inflation of the company's worth and understated its liabilities. This eventually contributed significantly to the company's downfall.

Referral Fees and Kickbacks

Kickbacks and referral fees, unlike related party transactions, are almost always viewed negatively and thus are often outlawed completely in certain industries. Neither shareholders, customers, nor fellow executives appreciate when a decision may have been arrived at because of a hidden and undisclosed relationship or reward.

Boards and officers can get involved in kickback schemes with companies that do work for them. In the 1990s, for instance, shareholders of a Pennsylvania company accused the CEO of taking kickbacks from a law firm that had done millions of dollars of work for the company.[22] More recently, the Federal Deposit Insurance Corporation (FDIC) and Housing and Urban Development (HUD) investigated a director of a Massachusetts bank for violations of the Real Estate Settlement Procedures Act. The government alleged that the board member and other defendants were providing baseball tickets and restaurant gift certificates to companies that sent them business.[23]

Arm's Length Transactions

Arm's length transactions are tied in closely with related-party transactions. A transaction that is made at "arm's length" is one that is "of or relating to dealings between two parties who are not related or not on close terms and who are presumed to have roughly equal bargaining power."[24]

A true arm's length transaction is when the parties are independent of each other, without some sort of special relationship, like being family members. However, it is possible to have a transaction between related parties that is handled as if it were at arm's length and that is thus acceptable.

Examples of transactions that may indicate a non–arm's length transaction are:

- ► Loans made with unusually low interest rates
- ► Loans made with insufficient paperwork
- ► Sales of real estate for lower than appraised value
- ► Paying too much or too little for supplies or equipment
- ► Unusual revenue streams at the end of a reporting period

THE ROLE OF THE BOARD OF DIRECTORS AS A WHOLE

The ultimate responsibility of the modern corporate director, individually and as part of the whole board, is the protection and growth of long-term shareholder value. There are several things directors must do to fulfill their responsibilities.

Directors Must Understand How Corporations Work

The board as a group has great powers, like appointing or removing executives and officers. One director may have little power or great influence, but in all cases directors have real accountability. Board actions are for the benefit of others—generally shareholders—and directors are judged on their actions for others. Directors must learn, over time, how corporations operate in general and they have a duty to be diligent in learning the unique aspects of how the company they serve as a director operates.

Directors Must Know What Acts to Avoid

Directors avoid gross negligence. In exercising their basic duties, directors do everything with a high standard of performance. More importantly, they attend to the basics of showing up to perform their duties, coming prepared for their work as directors, investing the time and energy required to properly handle their work, and exercising diligence in all they do. These actions will all help avoid charges of, or acts of, gross negligence.

Directors avoid conflicts of interest with the company they serve. They avoid competing directly or indirectly with the company they serve, and they avoid seizing corporate opportunities that belong to the company. They make themselves aware of any potential conflicts of interest with the company and immediately disclose even the hint of a conflict of interest, letting others review any potential conflicts to determine their propriety. Directors learn over their terms of service to avoid and properly manage other key areas of risk like properly addressing insider stock trading.

Directors Must Know Their Basic Responsibilities as Directors and Board Members

In exercising the duty of care, directors must be diligent and deliberate in handling all corporate matters. In exercising the duty of loyalty, directors must look after the interests of the stockholders, the company, and the many other stakeholders of the company including employees and customers. Directors must be aware of the handful of additional duties and standards in performing their duties like: the duty of candor in communicating for the company, the duty of confidentiality with boardroom deliberations, and the duty to disclose any conflicts or adverse interests they have with the company.

Directors Must Blend Diverse Attributes as a Cohesive Group Overseeing Management

Directors individually bring diverse attributes and experiences into the boardroom. Collectively, a board must come together as a cohesive group that works well together. Figure 2.3 gives a good view

FIGURE 2.3 Favored Attributes Differ Depending on Type of Board

	Public	Private	Nonprofit
Financial expertise	31.8	27.8	29.4
Specific industry experience	31.1	30.3	14.4
Leadership experience	29.1	28.5	39.4
Internat'l/global experience	16.0	9.9	3.9
Diversity	15.6	10.9	26.1
Strategy development	15.3	23.2	17.0
Corporate governance	9.6	15.1	9.6
Technological expertise	7.8	4.6	2.0
Information technology	6.2	2.8	2.8
Marketing	3.8	6.7	8.1
Risk assessment	3.6	4.2	1.5
Government experience	2.7	3.2	3.5
Medical/scientific expertise	2.0	2.8	3.9
Legal expertise	0.7	2.5	3.5
Human resources	0.4	0.7	2.0
Other	11.6	10.6	18.3

The NACD has published three surveys on public, private, and nonprofit companies that reveal attributes and experiences most important when recruiting directors. All three groups favor financial expertise, industry experience, and leadership, but they put different emphases on them.

Source: NACD Annual Surveys, 2013–2014.

of the favored attributes and experiences most desired by public, private, and nonprofit boards.

TOOLS AND TECHNIQUES FOR PROTECTING DIRECTORS FROM LIABILITY

A person who becomes a director or officer of a company, whether a for-profit or nonprofit company, opens him- or herself up to liability with regard to actions. Officers and directors are held to a duty of care as a standard and parties interested in the company often question whether this responsibility has been met when things go south.

Investors, employees, vendors, competitors, and customers, among others, may name officers and directors as defendants in lawsuits. Whether these lawsuits have merit or not, the cost of defending them is great.

To combat the threat of these suits and their repercussions—namely, an inability to find people willing to serve as directors and officers—companies often provide these individuals with directors and officers liability insurance (commonly referred to as "D&O").

D&O protects corporate directors and officers in the event they are personally sued, which typically happens in conjunction with the company being sued. The insurance provides protection by covering legal fees, settlements, judgments, and other costs. Although companies often have to pay a deductible, individual directors and officers do not have their own deductible.

If there are other high-level executives who are not officers or directors, the company can ask that they be included in the insurance for an additional premium. Sarbanes-Oxley has increased the liability risks of in-house accounting and legal personnel, so coverage is often added for these individuals.

The choice of defense counsel is generally left up to the directors or officers, subject to the company's approval. Given that defense costs can erode a policy's value pretty quickly, it is recommended that directors defend claims jointly instead of each having their own lawyers working independently. This may be impossible to the extent there are conflicts of interest or finger-pointing among board members.

Reasons for Providing Directors and Officers with Insurance

Given that directors and officers are sometimes sued personally because of things they allegedly do or do not do as directors and officers, they generally want protection from these suits before accepting the position and putting their personal assets at stake. Although companies often have general liability or umbrella business liability insurance policies, those generally do not provide protection from management liability lawsuits.

In addition to directors and officers being desirous of having insurance, investors such as venture capitalists and other financiers often require D&O as a condition of funding a company. The coverage is viewed as a way of protecting an investment.

Covered Claims and Costs

D&O liability policies cover "wrongful acts," which are generally defined in two parts:

- ► Alleged errors, misstatements, misleading acts, statements, omissions, or breaches of duties by officers or directors while acting in that capacity.
- ► Claims made against officers and directors solely because of their position as directors or officers.

The definition does not include claims arising from bodily injuries and property damage, those typically being covered by general liability insurance.

Some examples of claims often covered under D&O:

▸ Employment-related issues such as discrimination, harassment, and wrongful termination
▸ Failure to provide services
▸ Mismanagement of assets
▸ Lack of corporate governance

Claims of mismanagement of assets or funds are generally brought in what are called "derivative lawsuits." An individual, typically a shareholder, sues the director or officer on behalf of the organization because of harm done to the organization.

When the harm allegedly inflicted by the director or officer is not done to the organization as a whole, but to an individual, that individual brings the suit directly as opposed to derivatively. These "direct lawsuits" often relate to employment issues. Wrongful termination, sexual harassment, discrimination, and other employment practices are some of the largest sources of D&O liability claims.

Claims resulting in civil lawsuits are not the only ones that may be covered. D&O may also cover criminal, administrative, and regulatory proceedings, including investigations that may require the use of lawyers.

Covered Persons

D&O liability policies cover persons who:

▸ Have been directors and officers in the past.

- Are currently officers or directors.
- Will sometime in the future be officers or directors.

Coverage of past officers and directors is important because suits often arise well after the officers and directors have left their positions or have been terminated (the statute of limitations under Sarbanes-Oxley is five years). Coverage for future directors and officers is important so that they are not left without coverage if their company neglects to inform the insurer that the new officer or director has taken over at the position.

Companies That Need Directors and Officers (D&O) Liability Insurance

Publicly traded companies are the most common candidates for D&O liability insurance. The number of parties interested in the business, including shareholders, can be in the millions. Given the amount of money that publicly traded companies deal in, lawsuits may seek damages that make even the richest directors and officers fearful.

It is not unusual, however, for smaller business and nonprofits to provide D&O insurance. Although shareholders are a common source of suits against directors and officers, nontraded companies face many of the same issues.

Common Exclusions

While D&O liability policies typically cover defense expenses and financial damages or settlements, they generally do not cover wages, fines, taxes, penalties, or punitive damages. Further, while employment issues make up many of the claims against officers and directors, they are often excluded from coverage, necessitating a careful review of the policy by the purchaser.

Other common D&O liability insurance exclusions include:

- ► Illegal remuneration or personal profit
- ► Fraud
- ► Property damage and bodily harm
- ► Legal action already taken when the policy begins
- ► Claims made under a previous policy
- ► Claims covered by other insurance
- ► Claims made by one insured against another

There may be a general exclusion for misrepresentations made in the application for insurance or in the company's financial statements. The documents are not often submitted by directors and officers, so misrepresentations of others could lead to a lack of coverage for directors and officers. Some policies make exclusions *severable*, meaning wrongdoing that leads to exclusion for one officer or director will not lead to exclusion for anyone else.

Limits and Pricing

The maximum limits for D&O liability policies vary greatly. Smaller companies typically purchase policies with lower limits, while large companies might require limits in the hundreds of millions of dollars. Typical limits may be $500,000 to $1 million per claim.

Desired limits will affect pricing, as will the following common risk factors:

- Claims record
- Industry sector
- Amount of debt
- Profit
- Professional CVs of the management

The Three Sides of Directors and Officers (D&O) Liability Insurance

There are different types of D&O liability insurance, referred to as "sides," because at one point in time each part was put on a different side of a page. Most sides are now combined in the policy.

Side A

Side A D&O liability insurance (also referred to as "Coverage Part A") protects directors and officers from personal financial liability. Side A coverage generally only kicks in when the company is not indemnifying the directors and officers. The lack of indemnification might be because the company cannot afford to provide indemnification or because laws bar indemnification. Some states have laws prohibiting indemnification when a director has acted in bad faith or has otherwise failed to meet a certain behavioral threshold. The application of the indemnification laws can be difficult, often leaving directors unsure if Side A applies.

Side B

Side B is D&O liability insurance for the company. It comes into play when the company has losses due to indemnifying its officers and directors. In that way Side A and Side B complement each other. An example would be when a company pays a settlement or judgment rendered against its officers and directors after a shareholder derivative action.

Side C

Side C coverage is referred to as entity securities coverage. It covers the company when it is sued directly, beyond damages relating to indemnifying directors and officers. Side C coverage applies only to securities claims, as these claims represent the single largest threat to publicly traded companies.

Director Indemnification

One issue with D&O liability insurance is that once directors leave their board positions, they lose all control or input regarding the D&O policy, whether it be the limits of the policy or terms such as those that cover former directors.

Another way to protect directors is for companies to enter indemnification agreements with its directors. *Indemnification* is the process of agreeing or promising to pay for damages or losses that may occur in the future. In the boardroom context, companies may indemnify their directors by agreeing to pay their directors' litigation expenses and any damages should a lawsuit arise.

According to the Delaware Supreme Court, indemnification "serves the dual policies of (a) allowing corporate officials to resist unjustified lawsuits, secure in the knowledge that, if vindicated, the corporation will bear the expense of litigation; and (b) encouraging capable women and men to serve as corporate directors and officers, secure in the knowledge that the corporation will absorb the cost of defending their honesty and integrity."[25]

Corporate indemnification agreements are often set forth in the company's certificate of incorporation or bylaws, and are in some cases part of state law. Delaware, for instance, requires that companies pay the litigation expenses of directors who are successful in defending claims regarding their work as directors. Any further indemnification, however, such as the payment of judgments against the directors, is not required but is often allowed.

To qualify for indemnification, the director must meet a certain standard of conduct — it may be that of good faith, for instance, or acting with reasonable belief that the best interests of the corporation are being served. Whether this standard is met can generally only be determined after the litigation, so even indemnified directors must pay the costs of their defense in hopes that the amounts will be refunded by the company after litigation. D&O liability insurance may cover defense costs from the outset, however, and in some cases the company may advance defense costs to be refunded if the director is determined not to have met the requisite standard of care.

Another issue with indemnification is that companies may modify their bylaws or other corporate documents to remove or decrease the level of indemnification. In some states, a director's indemnification rights can vest with certain service time or in other circumstances.

A way to avoid the amendment pitfall is for directors to enter into an indemnification agreement that is *separate* from any general corporate documents. This arrangement would mean that any amendments would have to be approved by the director him- or herself, since he or she is a party to the contract.

Not all actions or claims are subject to indemnification. The SEC has stated that indemnification of directors for liabilities imposed by federal securities laws is against public policy and any such agreement is unenforceable.[26] The reasoning is that securities laws are intended to breed diligence and deter wrongdoing, and indemnification would undermine these objectives.[27]

NINE SIMPLE LOW-COST TIPS FOR LIABILITY PROTECTION

Sometimes simple and practical offers the best results, even in sophisticated situations like protecting yourself from potential liability in the boardroom. Here are nine effective ways to provide yourself with liability protection for any board you join. These tips could save you millions of dollars in liability and heartache.

1. The Estate Plan

Some of the simplest and best liability protection you can ever have is in your hands and can be implemented for next to nothing practically overnight. It is called an "estate plan" and involves the simple routine use of trusts. But you have to act. And you have to properly title your assets in the name of your trust for your estate plan to be fully effective. A trust only protects property properly transferred into the name of the trust.

If you are on a board and your estate plan is incomplete, without trusts implemented and properly funded, don't go home tonight without calling your estate attorney. Almost finished doesn't count when it comes to your estate plan, so no more delays if you need a plan.

2. Ask About Directors and Officers (D&O) Coverage

Don't be shy in asking about D&O coverage for any board you join. It is far better to know if there is no coverage. And if there is not, don't be afraid to ask why not, as you might learn something interesting or important about the people and board you are looking to join, including their worldviews on taking risks and running a business in general.

If there is coverage, ask for details on the amount. Ask to talk with the company's risk manager or insurance broker if the insurance seems inadequate. And don't be afraid to ask about the value of having more D&O liability coverage. That is exactly what my client Mary did. She was retiring from years as partner with a top accounting firm and was an independent director prospect any company would be lucky to have. A renowned private family business, heavy into manufacturing, was eager to have her join their board and several of the current independent directors were especially interested in her deep accounting and manufacturing industry experience.

The company and industry was not without its challenges. Still, Mary was pragmatic about the great opportunity before her and knew that joining her first prominent board was likely a fast track to her goal of serving on several boards in the next phase of her career. So Mary did her due diligence. Everything met her comfort level, except for the lack of clear answers on her questions about D&O liability coverage.

The other independent directors told Mary their D&O liability coverage was more than sufficient. The CEO said so as well. When Mary called in a favor and pinned down the chief financial officer (CFO) for a straight answer, she found there was only $1 million of D&O liability coverage, and the CEO was considering dropping that coverage.

Mary told the key independent directors she would love to join the board but wondered why they only carried $1million in coverage and asked if they could secure more. They believed there was some $10 million or more in coverage, and were actually shocked to confirm what Mary had discovered.

It turns out the CEO was a Warren Buffett devotee who lived to emulate all things Buffett. Directors at Buffett's Berkshire Hathaway are not provided D&O liability insurance, so the CEO took this as a reason to quietly cut back D&O liability coverage to $1 million to reduce expenses.

Mary joined the board with a special appreciation from the serving directors for a great catch, and they now benefit from $15 million in D&O liability coverage.

3. Look Left, Look Right, and Look Across the Table

The best protection you have comes from the ethics, integrity, and character of the other directors and officers seated with you at the boardroom table, and how they will respond when trouble shows up. Will the directors stand their ground no matter the challenge or personal cost, or will they head for the exit at the first sign of trouble?

Don't be naïve in joining a board. Trouble always shows up, whether it is routine matters like employment, pension, or discrimination claims, or complex matters like class action suits, hostile takeover activity, or derivative shareholder lawsuits.

Back to Buffett, at Berkshire Hathaway directors are expected to act like owners. If they screw up in managing shareholders' money, Buffett wants them to lose their money as well. Of course, Berkshire Hathaway directors hold more than $3 billion in shares, and no doubt they do their job with a keen interest.[28]

4. Don't Exclude the Exclusions in Your Review

Review all insurance policy exclusions. Invite the company's general counsel, risk manager, or agent selling the policy to walk the board of directors through the exclusion pages of your current insurance policies. At a minimum, it will be a great bit of continuing education. Often it is a wake-up call regarding the vital importance of how to handle key duties and responsibilities for every company director and executive. These reviews often lead to added insurance, broader coverage, or new policies.

5. Review the Right to Indemnify and Include Indemnity Protection

Most often you find any indemnity protection clauses in articles of incorporation or bylaws. Ask the CEO or general counsel to provide you and the board of directors with a presentation on any indemnity protections for the board, including a careful summary of how they work and the specific protection they offer.

6. Make the Minutes Count When Standing Alone or "Betting the Farm"

Never take board minutes for granted. When voting "no" or opposing a vote, vote "no" with enthusiasm. On bet the farm matters, take the liberty to instruct the person keeping the record and minutes to place any exact statement you like in the minutes. On especially important matters, review the record and minutes for accuracy after they are prepared for the permanent record to be sure it matches what transpired.

7. Watch Out for Those Payroll Tax Blues

Ask the auditors how they confirm payment of payroll taxes. Simply asking them makes them look twice. It is the first place companies skimp when cash is tight, especially nonprofits, and unpaid payroll taxes is one area where the Internal Revenue Service (IRS) will not yield in discharging directors from personal liability.

8. Don't Be Sleazy, Don't Be Sloppy, and Follow the Business Judgment Rule [29]

Do not be naïve when it comes time to join your first board. If needed, do some homework with your business lawyer or the board's corporate counsel on those basic topics of duty of care, duty of loyalty, and the Business Judgment Rule.

9. Reputational Risk

Reputations are invaluable. Keep that top of mind in all you do related to any boardroom service and it will provide great benefit to your service.

YOUR FIRST BIG CITY BOARD MEETING AND A MAJOR TEST

The day has finally arrived. After decades of hard work and great success, you have joined your first Fortune 500 company board.

Your first board meeting has been all you hoped it would be—stimulating, exciting, and a thrilling experience all in the rarified air of a spectacular location.

Your anxiety level is rising as the CEO moves into the next agenda item of the day. The CEO advises that an acquisition—so far confidential—has moved into high gear, given competitive threats. Time is of the essence to acquire this hot new product that everyone in the industry wants.

The CEO invites his or her senior management team to make the case for the multibillion-dollar acquisition. Next up are the finest acquisition consultants in the country, followed by the top investment bankers. Then it's the Wall Street lawyers. All strongly support doing the deal—now. The CEO suggests a break before board discussion and a vote on the acquisition.

As you head for the break, you face a quandary. You have deep knowledge of this product and technology. You have always questioned its future. The speed of this meeting has caught you off guard. It's obvious the CEO, his team and advisors are for the deal. The directors you chat up at break say it sounds great, and the CEO really knows how to make things happen. The chairman calls the directors back into the room stating, "Time to vote on our next billion-dollar deal."

You are stunned when there is minimal discussion and a motion is made to approve the deal. Hands shoot up around you with the "All in favor." You know you want to speak and ask a number of questions, but you are having trouble finding your voice. And you are wondering if you really want to be the skunk at the garden party on your first day in the boardroom.

Questions

1. What do you do or say when the chairman calls your name to vote?
2. Do you feel comfortable abstaining or are there other remedies?
3. Is this about loyalty, care, independence, or something else?
4. Were this a true case, what do you think would really happen?

What Really Happened at Your First Big City Board Meeting

So what really happened at the first big city board meeting? After final presentations, the board voted in favor with one dissenting vote. The lone dissenter was in his first board meeting. He carefully listened to all, asked a few astute questions, and quietly voted "no." When challenged he politely explained his reasons. The meeting moved to other minor business and wrapped up late. The CEO was peeved with his new director.

That night the CEO gave some thought to what the new director had said. He reached out to the director for a long early breakfast to explore his concerns. The director was a physician with deep knowledge of the new product and technology that was in the medical device space. The CEO listened, pursued the genuine concerns his team had missed or ignored, and ultimately led the board in reversing course, thus avoiding what became a major failure across his industry.

This is one of my favorite examples of moral courage as told by a renowned CEO. His company dodged a major failure. One independent-minded person can, at the right time and place, make a difference. It also tells the story of a CEO with a remarkable ability to listen, hear, and be fully aware of his world.

Chapter 3

THE ROYAL ROAD TO EXEMPLARY DIRECTORSHIP

The board for a corporation typically is authorized by, and derives its power through, state statutes and laws. The corporation's shareholders elect the board and it is charged with the obligation to act in the best interests of the shareholders and the corporation.

The board of directors of any corporation is legally responsible by statute, articles of incorporation, and bylaws, for the overall direction of the affairs, business, and operating performance of that corporation. The articles of incorporation and the bylaws are often known as the "organic, operating, or controlling documents" of the company.

The *articles of incorporation* tend to cover basic information about the corporation, like name, location, and business purpose. The *bylaws* cover the rules and regulations that govern the basic functions of the corporation, like the election, duties, and responsibilities of the company's directors and officers.

Beyond these basic controlling legal documents, we have the question: "How does a board best do the work of fulfilling its responsibilities to the company and its shareholders?" The answer most often is through the effective use of committees.

The structure of the board and the planning of the board's work are key elements to effective governance. Establishing committees is one typical way of managing the work of the board, thus supporting the board's governance role. Of course, having strong board leadership—with the CEO, board chairperson, and lead director being top talents—is vital to supporting the board's governance role as well.

Is every board required to have committees? Generally, yes, but technically not always. The boards of publicly traded companies on the major stock exchanges, like the New York Stock Exchange (NYSE) and the NASDAQ, are required as part of exchange corporate governance guidelines and standards to meet specific committee independence requirements. These requirements call for three independent committees: audit, compensation, and nominating and corporate governance. All must be comprised of directors that meet the required definitions for independence.

This has the effect of limiting executive and management influence over these critical functions. Top officers may use their powers of persuasion, but they don't get a vote. The public company shift to only independent directors for these key committees has played subtly in boardrooms. Over the years, these three committees have become the major operating committees for many boards.

In the public company setting, most boards typically have a handful of other committees beyond the three required committees of audit, compensation, and nominating and governance. Examples of other public company board committees include technology or IT, finance, capital, strategy, risk, management development, corporate social responsibility, compliance, and more.

Beyond the regulatory requirements for public company boards that require audit, compensation, and nominating and governance committees, there is no recommended structure or number of committees for a board to do its work. The range and type of committees are only limited by the imagination and creativity of the leadership involved.

Many public companies have a stock or equity awards committee. Their authority typically includes the declaration of dividends, authorization of the issuance of stock within board-approved limitations, administration of the dividend reinvestment plan, and implementation of share repurchase plans, all in accordance with board-approved capital plans. Often, these committees consist of a single company officer like the chief executive officer (CEO), the chief financial officer (CFO) or the general counsel.

The public company HP or Hewlett-Packard Company listed five board committees in 2013: audit, finance and investment, HR and compensation, nominating and governance, and as you might expect for HP, technology. Amgen, another public company, listed five board committees in 2013: audit, compensation and management, corporate responsibility and compliance, equity award, and governance and nominating.

In the private company setting, though many boards make great use of committees in conducting their work, it is possible for the owners to operate without the use of board committees. I have worked with a number of large privately held companies with up to a billion dollars in annual revenues that have boards comprised entirely of senior operating executives from the company that serve as directors. They function without any formal board committee structure, and no board committee is required by their articles of incorporation or bylaws. Typically, these companies have bylaws that permit committees, but do not require them.

In the nonprofit world, not all boards require committees to manage their work, though most make active use of committees. These might include finance or audit, key projects like strategic planning or a capital campaign, or some special work like a CEO search committee.

Nonprofit legal documents often reference two categories of board committees, standing committees and ad hoc committees. *Standing committees* are typically the long-term permanent committees named in the bylaws that manage the regular ongoing work like finance and audit. *Ad hoc committees* are typically established by the board on an as needed basis for a particular task or time line, like managing a major construction project or during an anniversary celebration year. They disappear when the task or event is completed.

The nonprofit world is also where you tend to see the largest number of committees used over the years. That's unsurprising when you consider how nonprofits recruit and use volunteers, deal with professional groups, and interact with a wide range of organizations like museums, colleges, and churches. The largest number of committees I have seen is 14 for a major health care system that included committees on government relations, community benefits, development or fund-raising, cultural diversity, marketing and communications, and quality.

There is a key caution to keep in mind for every director regarding committees. Using committees does not in any way limit the responsibility or liability of the board as a whole for the work performed by a committee. While using committees allows for the delegation of responsibility and can help manage the workload of the board as a whole, never presume as a director that handing work off to a committee in any way passes or limits liability to only those directors serving on a particular committee. Thus, the audit committee may oversee the work of financial reporting and the completion of the independent audit, but the whole board has full responsibility for these tasks.

Some other key points to consider with committees:

► A strong board committee structure is a great tool commonly used by boards to manage the workload and enhance governance.

► Beyond the required committees for public companies, certain other committees are also often found within these boards (finance committees on 19.5 percent of boards, risk committees on 13.1 percent of boards and strategic planning committees on 7 percent of boards).[1]

► Private company boards make heavy use of audit and compensation committees while nonprofit boards regularly have active nominating and governance, audit, and finance committees.

► The whole board has full fiduciary duty for all the work of the board even when there are committees handling much of the board's work.

(Continued)

> ▶ Committees expand and extend the capacity of the board to perform its work, but should never restrict key conversations the full board needs in key areas or in a time of crisis. The whole board best tackles key issues like strategy and CEO succession.

> ▶ Rotating chairs and board members onto new committees every few years can grow a director's knowledge and experience. Some directors don't need the added experience and others best serve the board as perhaps a long-standing audit or compensation committee chair.

> ▶ Committee chairs can enhance their roles substantially by staying connected to the board chair and other committee chairs. It also adds great value when a board chair knows the talents of all board members and selectively reaches out to noncommittee members to seek their input or to keep them advised on key matters.

THE IMPACT OF SARBANES-OXLEY ACT (SOX) AND DODD-FRANK ACT ON BOARD COMMITTEES

The world of corporate governance changed profoundly with passage of the Sarbanes-Oxley Act (SOX) of 2002 (and later amended) and the Dodd-Frank Wall Street Reform and Consumer Protection Act of 2010 (Dodd-Frank Act).

These extensive corporate governance regulations are for the most part only required of public companies. But they reverberated in private and nonprofit companies as well.

Two leading authorities say board governance has changed markedly over the past decade, and generally for the better. Rajiv "Raj" Gupta and Rochelle "Shelly" Lazarus spoke on the topic in a 2013 webcast sponsored by The Conference Board. Gupta and Lazarus both have years of CEO and director experience. Gupta's board experience includes Hewlett-Packard Company (HP), The Vanguard Group, and Tyco International. Lazarus has served as a board member for General Electric & Co. (GE), Merck & Co., and The Blackstone Group.

Gupta said public company boards today are far more diverse (though still not diverse enough). Boards are more independent and CEOs in no way control or manage the boards or appointment of directors. Lazarus concurred and told the story of serving on a board many years ago when every presentation was carefully scripted and any executive daring to deviate was immediately collared by the CEO. Lazarus said those meetings invited directors to take a snooze.

BOARD TOOLS AND STRUCTURES TO IMPROVE COMMITTEE PERFORMANCE

Boards have a fairly common range of tools available to them to enhance their performance including policies, manuals, guidelines, and charters.

Policies and Manuals

Some companies elect to regularly update comprehensive policies and store them in a common board manual or board policy manual. Many do not. When the board elects to have policies they can cover a wide range of topics. Typical board policies can include mission and vision statements, financial policies like limits on borrowing or debt capacity or spending authorization limits, committee definitions and descriptions, and criteria for new board members.

Some companies use a board policy manual as their primary tool for educating prospective directors and orienting new directors. A typical board policy manual might have five parts:

► Part 1. Orientation
► Part 2. Administrative Matters
► Part 3. Board Structure, Process, and Policies
► Part 4. Board and Management Relationships
► Part 5. Executive Powers and Limitations

There can be great value for the board and many benefits from having an organized tightly written board manual that places policies in a common location. Benefits include limiting duplication when new issues arise, providing the CEO and management clear direction in key policy areas, and setting a standard for organizational efficiency.

Corporate Governance Guidelines and Charters

Corporate governance guidelines typically are broad statements adopted by the board of directors of a company to represent the basic principles that govern the board in its oversight of the company. These guidelines are subject to the requirements of the company's charter and bylaws, as well as any other applicable law. They are best considered a working document to be reviewed by the board on a periodic basis for modification.

As a board tool, corporate governance guidelines establish and reflect a set of common expectations to assist the board and its committees in fulfilling their responsibilities to the company shareholders and stakeholders. Public companies are required to adopt and disclose corporate governance guidelines that cover qualification standards for directors, director responsibilities, director access to management, director compensation, director continuing education, evaluation of the board, and more. These guidelines must be published and available on the company's website.

The company's website must include its corporate governance guidelines. The proxy statement or annual report on Form 10-K must state that such guidelines are available on the website and provide the website address.[2] Typically you can find the following governance documents included there:

- Corporate Governance Guidelines
- Code of Business Conduct
- Corporate Governance Committee Charter
- Compensation Committee Charter
- Audit Committee Charter
- Related-Party Transactions Policy and Procedures
- Financial Code of Ethics

SPECIFIC COMMITTEES IN ACTION

These include audit committees, compensation committees, nominating and governance committees, special committees, and executive committees.

Audit Committees

Historically the audit committee has been the first among equals when it comes to board committees. The audit committee often was considered the committee that the board relied on to get the financial numbers right, the committee that required the greatest time commitment, and served as a training ground for many new directors to pay their dues and learn the business. It normally included the most senior members of the board with strong financial talent who could stay on top of the business.

With the fall of major public companies—like WorldCom, Adelphia Communications Corporation, Enron, and Lehman Brothers—and financial failure or crisis with many more—like HealthSouth—there has been a flood of new regulatory requirements imposing huge time demands from auditors, company accounting professionals, and company directors in financial reporting and compliance.

Today, the time requirements for audit committees remain so demanding that New York Stock Exchange (NYSE) rules limit the number of public company board audit committees one person can serve on to three. That comes with the added requirement that each board must determine that such simultaneous service would not impair the director's service and make public that finding.

Top audit committee members are in demand for the specialized skills they bring in financial management, financial reporting, and financial controls. Often they have deep experience, having served as chief financial officers or are former audit partners from the public accounting industry.

The specific requirements for audit committee members have expanded in recent years to a heavy focus on director independence, financial expertise, and overall financial literacy. Section 301 of the

Sarbanes-Oxley Act (SOX) requires that public companies listed on the national securities exchanges have audit committees comprised only of independent directors.

Director independence rules for the NYSE spell out that a director lacks independence if:

- The director is or has been in the last 3 years an employee of the listed company.
- The director has an immediate family member who is or has been an executive officer of the listed company.
- The director or an immediate family member has received direct compensation over 12 months of more than $120,000 in the last 3 years.
- The director or family member has close ties as a partner or former employee of the listed company's internal or external auditor.
- The director or an immediate family member has been employed as an executive of another company where any of the listed company's present executive officers at the same time serves or served on that company's compensation committee.
- The director is a current employee or a family member is CEO of a company that has sales, payments, or purchase transactions greater than 2 percent of the other listed company's consolidated gross revenues or $1 million.

Director independence rules for the NASDAQ Stock Market are similar.

Financial expertise and the concept of financial literacy are closely related. For decades, governance experts debated the benefit of requiring some or all of the directors of a company to possess a high level of financial literacy. Some made the case that all directors must be financially literate. As with director independence the Securities and Exchange Commission (SEC), in response to SOX, developed rules defining an audit committee financial expert and thus introducing that term into a framework required of all publicly traded companies.

The American Institute of Certified Public Accountants (AICPA) is particularly sensitive to this need as a result of the Sarbanes-Oxley Act of 2002 and the related SEC rules that place certain requirements on the audit committee of boards of directors that had not been there before. The SEC defines the *audit committee financial expert* as a person who has the following attributes:

► An understanding of generally accepted accounting principles (GAAP) and financial statements
► The ability to assess the general application of such principles in connection with the accounting for estimates, accruals, and reserves
► Experience preparing, auditing, analyzing, or evaluating financial statements that present a breadth and level of complexity of accounting issues that can reasonably be expected to be raised by the registrant's financial statements or experience actively supervising one or more persons engaged in such activities
► An understanding of internal controls and procedures for financial reporting
► An understanding of audit committee functions

In Figure 3.1 you will find a Financial Expert Decision Tree from the *AICPA Audit Committee Toolkit* that gives a good picture and map to help determine who qualifies as a financial expert.

FIGURE 3.1 Financial Expert Decision Tree

Has the person completed a program of learning in accounting or auditing?

NO

Does the person have experience as a principal financial officer, principal accounting officer, controller, public accountant, or auditor?

NO

Does the person have experience in one or more positions that involve the performance of similar functions?

NO

Does the person have experience actively supervising a person(s) performing one or more of these functions?

NO

Does the person have experience overseeing or assessing the performance of companies or public accountants with respect to the preparation, auditing, or evaluation of financial statements?

NO

Does the person have other relevant experience?

YES

In connection with education or experience, does the person have each of the following attributes?

1. An understanding of generally accepted accounting principles (GAAP) and financial statements.

AND

2. The ability to access the general application of such principles in connection with the accounting for estimates, accruals, and reserves.

AND

3. Experience preparing, auditing, analyzing, or evaluating financial statements that present a breadth and level of complexity of accounting issues that can reasonably be expected to be raised by the company's financial statements, or experience actively supervising one or more persons engaged in such activities.

AND

4. An understanding of internal controls and procedures for financial reporting.

AND

5. An understanding of audit committee functions?

YES

Candidate **meets the statutory requirements** to be identified as the audit committee financial expert.

NO

Candidate **does not meet the requirements** to be designated as the audit committee financial expert.

The AICPA developed this simple decision tree to determine if a candidate qualifies as a financial expert.

Source: The AICPA Audit Committee Toolkit (2010)

Key Work of the Audit Committee

The minimum technical requirements for a public company audit committee are daunting and extensive. In lay terms, the key responsibilities for good reporting and to satisfy the regulators include:

▶ Assure the independence of audit committee members.

▶ Direct the work of the registered public accounting firm they hire as the external auditor, including monitoring their ongoing independence.

▶ Receive and review all reports provided by both the external auditors and management.

▶ Comply with all stock market and SEC regulatory requirements, including reviewing the audited financial statements with management and recommending to the board of directors that the audited financial statements be included in the company's Form 10-K.

The audit committee charter is a vital tool in organizing the work of the audit committee. It summarizes the roles and responsibilities of the committee and outlines its scope, structure, and processes. A typical audit committee charter includes sections on:

▶ The purpose, charge, and authority of the committee

▶ The membership of the committee, including qualifications with a focus on independence, the work and role of the chairman, and removal of members

▶ The procedures, which could include the number of meetings required; agenda management; right to call executive session; authority to retain advisors; annual review of charter;

performance review of committee; and right to full access to accountants, executives, records, and books

▶ The responsibilities of the audit committee

Typical common key responsibilities of audit committees include:

▶ **Audit and Nonaudit Services.** Oversee the audit and nonaudit services of the public accounting firm and manage all the relationships of the firm with the company.

▶ **Annual Audit and Quarterly Statements.** Meet to review with management and accounting firm the annual audit and quarterly financial statements.

▶ **Earnings Releases.** Review all earnings press releases, company policies on financial information, and earnings guidance.

▶ **Disclosure Controls.** Review the adequacy and effectiveness of company disclosure controls and procedures. (*Note:* Many companies have a special disclosure committee to keep up with this important task.)

▶ **Regulatory and Accounting Initiatives.** Review the impact of any new regulatory and accounting initiatives, including any off-balance sheet legal or financial structures. (*Note:* "Off-balance sheet" financing vehicles were one of the key elements in the demise of Enron, so it is very important to learn about, understand, and monitor these.)

▶ **Internal Controls.** Review the adequacy and effectiveness of internal controls.

▶ **Complaints.** Oversee procedures established to fulfill the handling of direct and anonymous submissions of complaints and alleged violations of securities laws, auditing matters, and other concerns. (*Note:* This is commonly known as the "Whistleblower" function.)

▶ **Risk.** Oversee risks the company faces and management's approach to address and mitigate these risks. Figure 3.2

FIGURE 3.2 Key Steps in Developing a Risk Appetite Statement

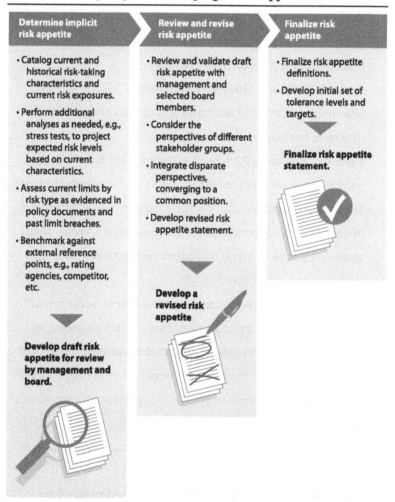

Determine implicit risk appetite	Review and revise risk appetite	Finalize risk appetite
• Catalog current and historical risk-taking characteristics and current risk exposures.	• Review and validate draft risk appetite with management and selected board members.	• Finalize risk appetite definitions.
• Perform additional analyses as needed, e.g., stress tests, to project expected risk levels based on current characteristics.	• Consider the perspectives of different stakeholder groups.	• Develop initial set of tolerance levels and targets.
• Assess current limits by risk type as evidenced in policy documents and past limit breaches.	• Integrate disparate perspectives, converging to a common position.	**Finalize risk appetite statement.**
• Benchmark against external reference points, e.g., rating agencies, competitor, etc.	• Develop revised risk appetite statement.	

Develop a revised risk appetite

Develop draft risk appetite for review by management and board.

Developing a risk management statement is an important step in an effective risk management program

Source: Risk Governance: Balancing Risk and Reward by NACD.

details how to develop a risk management statement. (*Note:* Using separate risk committees is a step that some companies elect to use. Regulators talk of pursuing mandatory risk committees for companies with major risks in key industries like banking.)

▶ **Compliance, Internal Audit, Director of Internal Audit, Attorney Reports, and more.**

There is a terrific article that provide provides a wealth of insights and I recommend it to you: "Eight Habits of Highly Effective Audit Committees: Tools to Take Your Committee to the Next Level" by John F. Morrow and Joan Pastor in the *Journal of Accountancy*, September 2007.

Top Resources for the Audit Committee

Resources for operating an effective audit committee are bountiful. The top accounting firms and auditors have a long tradition of educating their clients with terrific educational resources. Now, more than ever, the role of the audit committee is critical to organizational effectiveness.

Here are several excellent resources for those looking to quickly come up to speed on audit committees:

▶ **From The National Association of Corporate Directors (NACD).** *Report of the Blue Ribbon Commission on the Audit Committee: Overview and Recommendations.* The NACD has for decades issued Blue Ribbon Commission reports on key topics.

▶ **From the American Institute of Certified Public Accountants (AICPA).** The *AICPA Audit Committee Toolkit.*

This series was developed by AICPA's Business, Industry and Government Section to help audit committees achieve best practices for managing and incorporating their role in the organization. Each Toolkit offers a broad sampling of check-lists, matrices, reports, questionnaires, and other pertinent materials designed to make audit committee best practices actionable. Each is revised and updated, as needed, to respond to emerging issues, trends, and risks. There are Toolkits available for private companies, public companies, government organizations, and not-for-profit organizations.

► **From the Institute of Internal Auditors (IIA) Research Foundation and PricewaterhouseCoopers (PwC).** *Audit Committee Effectiveness—What Works Best,* 4th edition. This book was a joint project by the IIA Research Foundation, a foundation that strives to set the standard for professional achievement in the internal auditing profession and PwC, one of the world's largest assurance, tax, and advisory service firms.

► **From KPMG's Audit Committee Institute (ACI).** The Annual Audit Committee Issues Conference. KPMG—another of the world's largest assurance, tax, and advisory service firms—has an active Audit Committee Institute that is focused on supporting audit committees and boards with resources and peer-exchange opportunities on the topics of financial reporting, audit quality, and challenges facing business. Their programs include the Annual Audit Committee Issues Conference, webcasts, and many other resources.

Many of the other accounting, legal, and professional service firms provide educational programs geared toward financial reporting, auditing, and audit committees as do many of the college- and university-based executive education programs on accounting, auditing, and governance.

Several great resources and their websites for those wanting more on audit committees include The Institute of Internal Auditors (www.theiia.org), the American Institute of Certified Public Accountants' Audit Committee Effectiveness Center (www.aicpa .org/ForThePublic/AuditCommitteeEffectiveness/Pages/ACEC .aspx), the Committee of Sponsoring Organizations of the Treadway Commission (COSO) (www.coso.org), and the National Association of Corporate Directors (www.nacdonline.org).

A good current book for the new audit committee member is *The Board of Directors and Audit Committee Guide to Fiduciary Responsibilities: Ten Critical Steps to Protecting Yourself and Your Organization*, by Sheila Moran and Ronald Krol, available from AMACOM, 2013.

A good current book for the deeply engaged advanced audit committee member is *Audit Committees Portfolios* by Frederick D. Lipman, Barry H. Genkin, and Yelena Barychev, available from Bloomberg BNA (Bureau of National Affairs, Inc.), 2013.

Great Questions for the Audit Committee to Remember

One of the most important responsibilities for all board members is to ask penetrating and insightful questions. This is vital in the case of the audit committee. Since directors spend relatively little time dealing with affairs of the company, as compared to management, they cannot be expected to possess a comparable level of knowledge. However, they can, and should, be expected to ask probing questions about management's proposals and actions.

Warren Buffett has cast a critical eye at audit committees. He observes the obvious by stating: "Audit committees can't audit. Only the company's outside auditor can determine whether the earnings that a management purports to have made are suspect." He states that many managers fudge numbers in ways that might be legal but can materially mislead investors, and auditors often play along.

Buffett suggests that no matter what the rules say about the auditors working for the board, the CFO and CEO pay their bills and have a big influence on them. Thus, he recommends that audit committees put auditors on the spot with four tough questions:

1. If the auditor were solely responsible for preparation of the company's financial statements, would they have in any way been prepared differently from the manner selected by management? This question should cover both material and nonmaterial differences. If the auditor would have done something differently, both management's argument and the auditor's response should be disclosed. The audit committee should then evaluate.

2. If the auditor were an investor, would he have received—in plain English—the information essential to his understanding the company's financial performance during the reporting period?

3. Is the company following the same internal audit procedures that would be followed if the auditor himself were the CEO? If not, what are the differences and why?

   Is the auditor aware of any actions—either accounting or operational—that have had the purpose and effect of moving revenues or expenses from one accounting period to another?

A top authority on securities law with deep experience in serving Silicon Valley companies, Boris Feldman of the firm Wilson Sonsini Goodrich & Rosati, produced a terrific list of questions for auditors found here.

Questions to Ask Your Auditors
- ► What is your degree of comfort with the company's accounting decisions? How would you characterize the company's aggressiveness/conservativeness relative to other companies in its industry? Relative to the most widely respected public companies?
- ► Which accounting treatments present the greatest risk of being questioned down the road?
- ► Do you think that the company is managing earnings to a particular target, rather than reflecting the true results of operations?
- ► Which accounting items tended to reflect judgment calls, rather than automatic counting?
- ► Did you perceive any changes in policies or practices from prior periods?
- ► Did you make any recommendations or suggestions that management did not accept?
- ► Are there any employees of the company that you felt were not entirely candid and responsive to you?
- ► If you were our internal chief accounting officer, would you have made any accounting decisions differently?

- ▶ Were there any accounting treatments as to which you consulted your national office?
- ▶ How would you assess the internal controls at the company? What improvements would you make? In what priority?
- ▶ Are the accounting personnel capable? Do they have integrity? Does the finance department have adequate staffing?
- ▶ Did you sense that management directs the finance personnel in making accounting decisions?
- ▶ What procedures did you use to test revenue recognition? Did you find any red flags?
- ▶ What procedures did you use to evaluate the reasonableness of reserves and accruals? Were there items for which you would have reserved a different amount?[3]

Compensation Committees

The Securities and Exchange Commission (SEC), the New York Stock Exchange (NYSE) and the NASDAQ Stock Market (the NASDAQ) require that publicly held companies have a compensation committee to address executive compensation and other related activities. The NYSE, for one, requires that the committee members be "independent," and states that a compensation committee must:

- ▶ Review and approve goals relevant to CEO compensation.
- ▶ Evaluate the CEO's performance in light of such goals.
- ▶ Determine and approve the CEO's compensation based upon such evaluation.

The role and importance of a board's compensation committee, and the scrutiny given to its decisions, have increased in recent years given the many corporate scandals and meltdowns in the first decade of the twenty first century. Public anxiety and concern have culminated in the following reform or other activity:

- The Dodd-Frank Wall Street Reform and Consumer Protection Act of 2010, which includes mandated "say on pay"—shareholders now must be given the opportunity to vote on executive compensation arrangements—and disclosure of "golden parachute" compensation arrangements
- Governance reform
- Increased shareholder activism and media scrutiny of executive compensation

Reform and public scrutiny of executive compensation has resulted in enormous pressure on boards to rein in or scale back compensation programs. Boards and compensation committees have to balance compensation scrutiny and ensure that the company remains competitive, all while complying with regulations.

There are three broad categories[4] of compensation committee responsibilities:

- **Strategic oversight of compensation programs.** This involves developing a compensation strategy, ensuring that current compensation plans are geared around that strategy, ensuring regulatory compliance regarding compensation plans, and keeping up with current compensation best practices.
- **Pay administration.** This aspect is more specific, including reviewing and deciding upon changes to a CEO's or other executive's compensation or to overall corporate compensation packages.

▶ **Other.** This involves developing a committee charter and amending as necessary, evaluating director compensation plans, and reviewing the Compensation Discussion and Analysis (CD&A) section of the company's Annual Report. In some instances, the committee may handle CEO evaluation and succession planning.

Of primary concern is that a compensation committee find out what the company is trying to achieve with compensation and make certain that the executive compensation packages in place are directed at meeting the company's compensation policy objectives. Having a compensation policy or program is a useful business tool, but the SEC also requires that companies describe such a policy (and thus they effectively must have one) in the Compensation Discussion and Analysis (CD&A) portion of their annual report/proxy statement. As for other disclosures by the committee, a company's Form 10-K must include a Compensation Committee Report which names the committee members and demonstrates approval of the company's CD&A.

Excessive compensation is perhaps the touchiest subject for compensation committees, and can lead to conflict with the CEO and director embarrassment should the press become bloodthirsty. For this and similar reasons, while the audit committee is seen as the most technical of the board committees, the compensation committee is seen as the most emotional.

However, while committees must be cognizant of excessive compensation, as long as they follow procedures, stay up on trends and industry standards, and do not act out of self-interest, regulators and courts will not find the committee to have committed any violations. Spending some time with a third-party compensation expert can go a long way to educating compensation committee members, and following the expert's recommendations may provide a level of assurance about the committee's actions. Though it can be hard for shareholders and the public in general to swallow, having competitive compensation programs is absolutely necessary to obtaining and retaining top talent.

Nominating and Governance Committees

Every publicly traded company should have an independent board committee that addresses director nominations and corporate governance issues (the two subjects are generally tackled by one committee).

Boards have long had committees set up to nominate director candidates for the rest of the board and for the corporation's shareholders. However, as corporate governance has become more of a focus in the boardroom, committees that once focused only on nominating directors added the related responsibility of overseeing the composition, structure, and evaluation of the board and its committees.

The committee's responsibilities include:[5]

- ► Identifying, evaluating, and recommending board member candidates to the board and to shareholders
- ► Providing orientation, direction, training, and continuing education programs for directors
- ► Developing and presenting to the board certain corporate governance principles
- ► Establishing criteria for board and board committee membership

▶ Evaluating the board and its members

▶ Determining or evaluating procedures for shareholder communications with the board

▶ Overseeing or assisting in succession planning both for the CEO and for board members

It is vital that the committee keep abreast of the evolving "best practices" in the corporate governance realm. One way to keep on top of governance policies is to constantly monitor the policies of competitors and similar-sized companies.

The committee should continually evaluate the board's committee structure. As the company and the economic and political atmosphere evolve, new committees will undoubtedly need to be created and certain committees may need to be dissolved. Committee qualifications are also important, as some committees require a particular level of independence or expertise (for instance, it might be important to have someone on the audit committee with accounting or financial experience).

The nominating and governance committee is responsible for seeing that the board functions properly and has proper guidelines in place for doing so. For instance, the committee should ensure that the board meets enough times, that there is a proper agenda in place for meetings, and that there is the framework for meaningful participation from board members and management present at the meetings.

In addition to facilitating boardroom participation, the governance committee should also evaluate actual participation by board members. Directors should work well with each other and with the CEO, and if they do not, the nominating and governance committee may need to think about changing the composition of the board.

Director positions should not be thought of as permanent. A candid conversation about evaluating and renominating current directors is an important part of what the nominating and governance committee must achieve.

Information flow is also an important part of a functioning board, and the governance and nominating committee should see that information channels are set up to work properly. One key is to ensure that the board and management can and do communicate to the extent necessary and that messages from one to the other are not garbled, misheard, or misread. The committee should see that the board has the proper channels to receive information from the press and outside analysts.

Director independence is becoming more and more of a hot button topic, and it is the nominating and governance committee's responsibility to ensure that the requisite number of directors is indeed independent. The committee itself should also maintain independence.

As for the "nominating" portion of the committee's duties, that committee should identify, evaluate, and recommend director candidates, utilizing its own sources and recommendations of shareholders and others. Developing appropriate criteria for board membership is integral in this process. Criteria may include experience, expertise, integrity, and others, and it is generally important that directors are chosen from diverse pools (different ages, races, genders, etc.).

A recent trend for nominating committees involves the use of a "board composition matrix," wherein desired skills or backgrounds to have in the board are listed on a matrix. The committee can note which of those items are fulfilled by the board and where gaps lie. The matrix should evolve with the company and the business environment.

Nominating committees often use outside search groups to assist in finding potential directors. These search firms can be useful, but it is important that the committee not lose control of the process.

Once a potential director is identified, he or she is usually brought in for an interview. Traditionally, once an interview was set up, an offer was expected. This has rightfully begun to change, as potential directors view interviews as an opportunity to see if the position is a good fit for them and boards get a feel for how or if the interviewee would satisfy the board's needs. It is important for boards to be selective, as it is not always easy to get rid of an ineffective director.

Special Committees

A board can form an independent committee to assist in carrying out any number of special projects or oversight responsibilities, including financing, budgeting, investment, risk management, and mergers and acquisitions.

When the term *special committee* is used in the world of corporate governance, it is usually referring to a need that has to be addressed. It could involve a special negotiation like a merger, a going private sale transaction, a special litigation like stockholder derivative litigation, a "bet the farm" problem, or a special investigation like some major alleged corporate fraud in the company or with the board. The need for a special committee often stems from a potential conflict of interest for some group within the board of directors or the risk of an interested party or related party transaction involving the board or management.

The use of a special negotiation committee can help establish fair dealing with the involved or interested parties. A highly publicized example of a special negotiation committee involved Michael Dell's successful 2013 attempt to take the public company Dell private.

Dell had formed a special board committee of independent directors while still a public company to negotiate with Dell, Silver Lake Partners, and others interested in purchasing Dell when the board learned of Michael Dell's intent to buy the company with Silver Lake Partners. Their work was intense and came under close scrutiny.

Special committees typically have no written board charter. They operate under some specific board resolution that lays out their mandated work, names the committee members, funds the work, and authorizes their duties and powers.

A highly publicized example of a special investigation committee came when Hewlett-Packard Company (HP) appointed a special board committee to investigate the 2011 acquisition of Autonomy Corporation. The purchase price was $11 billion, but the acquisition quickly turned into an $8.8 billion write-down amid claims of financial fraud. Three newer board members formed the special board committee. This write-down brought numerous lawsuits.

Board Committees for Several Types of Large Companies

Large Private Company: REI

- ► Executive Committee
- ► Nominating and Governance Committee
- ► Compensation Committee
- ► Audit and Finance Committee

Source: REI website board committees

Large Charity: AARP

- ► Audit and Finance Committee
- ► Compensation Committee
- ► Governance Committee
- ► Member and Social Impact Committee
- ► Nominating Subcommittee of Governance Committee
- ► National Policy Council (NPC)

Source: AARP website board committees

Large Medical Provider: Cleveland Clinic

- ► Audit Committee
- ► Compensation Committee
- ► Conflict of Interest and Managing Innovations Committee
- ► Development Committee
- ► Finance Committee
- ► Governance Committee
- ► Government and Community Relations Committee
- ► Research and Education Committee

> Safety, Quality and Patient Experience Committee

Source: Cleveland Clinic website board of directors and
board committees

Large University: Board of Visitors Committees for
the University of Virginia

> Advancement and Communications Committee

> Audit and Compliance Committee

> Buildings and Grounds Committee

> Educational Policy Committee

> Executive Committee

> Finance Committee

> Medical Center Operating Board Committee

> Student Affairs & Athletics Committee

> The University of Virginia's College at Wise
> Committee

> Special Committee on Diversity Committee

> Special Committee on Governance and Engagement
> Committee

> Special Committee on Strategic Planning Committee

Source: © 2014 Board of Visitors' Executive Committee,
Board of Visitors, University of Virginia website

Executive Committee: Yes or No?

Some boards make use of an executive committee, a smaller subset
of the entire board, such as the chairman of the board, the CEO,
and the chair of each committee. An executive committee can be
a productive tool for managing the work of the board in the right

circumstances. But a concern arises. Does the executive committee create a system that can divide the board between those directors actively engaged and those less involved?

Let's clarify that the term "executive committee" is distinct from a related term, "executive session." An *executive session* refers to the practice of the independent directors meeting without the CEO and executive team present. *Executive committee* refers to a smaller group of the entire board that has special rights and responsibilities, at times handling much of the regular workload for the board.

Executive committees can be effective when the chairman and board leadership use this tool to manage a heavy workload, is aware of the risk for divisiveness, and make special efforts to keep all directors fully informed and engaged. Executive committees can fail when a two-class system develops between those in the know on critical issues and those out of the loop. Typically, when the use of an executive committee creates a two-class system you do not get a power struggle. Rather, you end up with a group of disengaged directors who fail to provide robust service to the board at the level they could.

The actual use of executive committees by boards of all types tends to fall into three categories:

- ▶ Boards that do not use executive committees.
- ▶ Boards that actively use executive committees.
- ▶ Boards that operate without a regular executive committee, but reserve an executive committee for special circumstances, like managing a crisis or a major project.

Recent surveys by the National Association of Corporate Directors (NACD) show that 66 percent of nonprofit organization, 30 percent of private company, and 24 percent of public company boards have executive committees. I have seen boards thrive with executive committees and without them.

I offer two thoughts for you to consider:

▻ The recent developments with many boards actively using lead directors separate from the CEO may eliminate the need for executive committees. Under that scenario, the lead director can pick up some of the work covered by an executive committee. Likewise, many nominating and governance committees perform many of the functions of an executive committee.

▻ If a board using an executive committee has concerns that a two-class system is becoming a problem, there is a practical solution to diagnose the problem: simply ask the directors who are not part of the executive committee, in a confidential manner, if they believe their work and roles on the board are diminished by having an executive committee. Chances are high that you will get a straight answer on the value of having an executive committee and act accordingly.

If your board is functioning with an executive committee, be sure you have a clear understanding of the roles, responsibilities, and powers of the executive committee as it relates to the full board. Typically, there will be a clear simple statement of the powers involved. Here you will find two examples from public company JPMorgan Chase & Co. and the Board of Visitors for the University of Virginia.

Executive Committee for JPMorgan Chase & Co.
"The Board-level Executive Committee consists of Crandall C. Bowles, James S. Crown, James Dimon, Laban P. Jackson, Jr., Lee R. Raymond,

and William C. Weldon. It may exercise all the powers of the Board that lawfully may be delegated. The Board-level Executive Committee was established with the expectation that it would not take material actions absent special circumstances."[6]

Executive Committee for Board of Visitors, University of Virginia

"The Executive Committee shall consider all matters referred to it by the Rector, the Vice Rector, or the President and shall, in the interim between meetings of the Board, be vested with the powers and authority of the full Board and shall take such action on all matters that may be referred to it as, in its judgment, is required.

"All such actions taken by the Executive Committee in the interim between meetings of the Board shall require a two-thirds vote of the whole number of committee members, and their actions shall be reported to the Board at the next regular meeting and shall, if confirmation is required, be confirmed and approved by the Board at that time."[7]

Sample Public Company Board Guidelines and Structure

Corporate Governance Guidelines

These Corporate Governance Guidelines adopted by the Board of Directors of the Company represent the principles that govern the Board in its oversight of the affairs of the Company. These Guidelines are subject to the requirements of the Company's charter and bylaws, as well as applicable law, and may be modified from time to time as determined by the Board.

Board Responsibilities

The Board is responsible for promoting the best interests of the Company and its shareholders, while also considering those essential to the Company's success, namely its employees, customers, vendors, and communities. While management remains responsible for the Company's day-to-day operations and activities, the Board is responsible for monitoring the effectiveness of management's efforts.

Board Structure

Size of the Board

Director Criteria and Selection

Board Leadership

Director Change in Position and Other Directorships

Director Compensation and Share Ownership

Director Orientation and Education

Service of Former CEO on the Board

Director Retirement Age

Meetings of the Board of Directors

Frequency of Meetings

Executive Sessions of the Nonmanagement Directors

Information Flow

Board Effectiveness Review

(Continued)

Access to Management and Independent Advisors

Attendance of Nondirectors at Meeting

Committees of the Board

Number and Types of Committees

Frequency of Committee Meetings

Committee Agendas and Reports

Assignment and Rotation of Committee Members

Management Compensation and Succession

CEO Performance Evaluation and Compensation

Compensation of Other Executive Officers

Succession Planning

Communications with the Public

Source: Compilation of multiple public company board struc-ture and guideline documents including The Laclede Group, The Coca-Cola Company, and Tenet Healthcare Corporation.

OTHER BOARD/COMMITTEE EFFICIENCY ISSUES AND TOOLS

Board Portals

Board Portals are secure online forums intended to grant to a board of directors easy access to files and documents via off-site stor-age. Board Portals are not simple websites, they are encrypted to limit access and keep their content protected from casual browsers. Directors and other approved persons are allowed access through passwords or locally installed software. Portals can be custom-built by a company information technology (IT) department or purchased from third-party vendors.

Board Portals offer strict security and access control. Many use *two-factor authentication for logins*—often a password and a security question, or role-based access to secure information. Board Portal software is designed for fast and safe dissemination of information. Corporate secretaries can create and modify packets hosted on the portal. Any edits made to the packets are updated instantly. In the case of online collaborations, committee members can apply changes instantly, and track the contributions of others.

Board Portals allow both online and offline accessibility. Board members can download documents from the Board Portals to their personal computers or mobile devices. They can also access the same information and communication from anywhere in the world using the Internet. Files downloaded locally still support the same strict security as those hosted on the Board Portal, itself.

Board Portals allow secure communication between board members while keeping accurate records and tracking key performance indicators to allow directors to review board effectiveness and participation. Off-site storage provides a safe backup for sensitive files and documents, and ensures all board members have up-to-date and accurate information.

Board Portals offer another benefit that company lawyers like. Directors can make notes on their electronic board books with the knowledge that those notes will be permanently erased at some certain date, as determined by the company.

Handwritten notes can be inherently ambiguous and thus twisted by a plaintiff's lawyer to his or her purposes. Many a lawsuit deposition has involved hours of probing the meaning of a director's notes.

Minutes That Matter

Skillfully written minutes are essential in today's boardroom as an added tool and preventive technique to ultimately avoid routine director actions turning into courtroom nightmares and real director liability. Using skill and care in the drafting, review, and approval of minutes is vitally important today. While keeping minutes might be considered a mundane task by some, the reality is that well-crafted accurate minutes can be a great asset to any organization and provide invaluable protection to the directors should litigation or other adverse matters arise. A clear and concise record at the right time can be priceless for any director.

In recent years, litigation makes it clear that courts will look to boardroom and committee minutes when director conduct is under review. Nonexistent, erroneous, or vague minutes can be a real risk to directors today. A clear record of accurate minutes that credibly establishes past boardroom conduct can provide great comfort and real protection to directors if and when litigation shows up.

To put a fine point on the value of boardroom minutes I provide an invaluable quote:

> The primary purpose of minutes is to present a clear record of board or committee action taken. Minutes should be reasonably comprehensive and detailed as to action taken and discussion about such action. Directors must remember that when reviewing minutes: if an action is not reported in the minutes, for legal purposes, it will be difficult to establish that it happened. Courts will assume that an issue was not discussed or debated if the minutes do not reflect it. Thus, directors may lose the protections of the Business

Judgment Rule and could be held liable for violations of their fiduciary duties solely based on inaccurate or incomplete minutes. Therefore, minutes should reflect all decisions made, and should at least signal discussion of other topics addressed in the boardroom.[8]

I offer the following tips when it comes to board minutes. Minutes can be boring as dirt, but they can also sink your ship, so pay attention to these tips:

1. **Relax.** Chances are you will not be the one having to take the minutes. Companies of any real size will have legal counsel, management, or the corporate secretary normally handle these important details. By the time you are asked to keep the minutes, you will have gained experience, or can simply decline saying you would rather focus on the meeting in process.

2. **Read the minutes closely.** Many directors don't take the time to read the minutes closely. Whenever you take a personal stand in the boardroom on something important be sure to make a personal review of the minutes for accuracy. If you ever take an exceptional position in the boardroom, such as being the sole dissenter on an important vote, review the minutes for accuracy, and be sure to keep a copy for your personal records. Yes, rascals have been known to change the minutes and records in the permanent record to their benefit after they were approved. Corporate lore has it that a number of the serving directors tarnished by the collapse of Enron Corporation early on were suspicious of the rapid growth and highly complex financial transactions, particularly the "special

purpose entities" used to richly compensate CFO Andrew Fastow. The story goes that their "tip-off" came from noticing problems and inconsistencies with the compensation committee minutes. This is corporate lore I remind you, and for sure a day late and a dollar short given the collapse, but it makes my point on the importance of minutes. Of course, these were the same directors that voted twice on the record to suspend the Enron ethics policies to permit Fastow's participation in the "special purpose entities." Oh, never mind, this isn't the section on ethics.

3. **Have skilled attorney or corporate secretary take the minutes.** For complex organizations like public company boards, especially when dealing with key committees like audit or compensation, the level of detail truly requires legal judgment. It is best to simply assume that all minutes may one day be subpoenaed for a lawsuit or regulatory action, and thus warrant a skilled attorney or corporate secretary taking the minutes.

4. **Personal notes.** Personal notes of meetings are part of the record and will be subpoenaed if litigation shows up. Destroy them shortly after any meeting or discuss with company legal counsel how to handle them if you can't live without them.

5. **Minutes document the past.** They also make a great reference source for future use on the history and business of the company. You know you are with a buttoned-up organization when they go the extra mile to develop and maintain a comprehensive index of past minutes. Ask for this. It never hurts to ask.

Meetings, Attendance, and Procedures

A major distinction between good boards and great boards is how the directors work together productively as a group, or not. The best boards make great use of regular meetings of the full board to affirm the mission, clarify the vision, and discuss or debate strategy on a regular basis so that the directors, management, and the entire organization are on the same page over the long term.

Boards of directors are frequently more involved with rich dialogue and reaching consensus than getting to a vote. Make an effort to learn early on the style and approach of the board in decision making when you enter a new boardroom.

Annual meetings are almost universally required for companies of all types with a key function of electing directors and officers for the coming year. Public companies and large nonprofits typically hold formal annual meetings, open to their shareholders or members and all who want to attend. Private companies and smaller nonprofits often hold informal annual meetings in the boardroom.

The legal requirements for meetings and attendance, like the days and method of notice can be precise and on occasion vitally important. Legal counsel, management, or the corporate secretary normally handle these important details. Attendance records for public company directors are routinely published today in the "notice of annual meeting" and are watched closely by institutional investors and others. Most companies today have legal provisions permitting directors to meet by telephone in many circumstances.

And what about Robert and his rules of order? Are they used in the boardroom on a regular basis and do I need to learn them? *Robert's Rules of Order* (named for Brig. Gen. Henry Martyn Robert, and dating back to 1876) are seldom used in the more informal atmosphere of corporate boardrooms. In my decades of experience in corporate boardrooms I have never encountered them, nor have any of my many peers. It is typical for large annual meetings to have some type of procedures or rules of order spelled out and about half of the public companies use *Robert's Rules of Order* for their annual meetings according to the Society of Corporate Secretaries & Governance Professionals Survey.

Most every boardroom has its rules of the road for running meetings. The rules frequently are unwritten, though occasionally they are written in a board policy manual. As you enter a new boardroom, it's good to watch for the rules of the road in action, or ask a confidant or board chair to educate you. If you are fortunate enough to have a director orientation, make the most of the training.

Orienting New Directors or "On-boarding"

Boardroom orientation for new directors can range from a few words of "welcome to the board" at your first meeting, to the assignment of a mentor or board buddy to teach you the ropes, to the provision of a detailed board manual along with an extended in-person orientation. Every board has a culture that is defined by its customs, traditions, and practices. Every new board member can benefit from an introduction to that culture—not just the ability to meet the general expectations placed on individual board members. I believe formal orientations are valuable.

Numerous resources are available for creating a good board member orientation program. Professional associations provide guidance and many boards have great tools that they are very willing to share upon request. The National Association of Corporate Directors (NACD) has, as part of their Director's Handbook Series, a title named *The Onboarding Book, 2012 Edition,* which is a terrific template for the orientation of new directors with many sample documents. BoardSource, a national organization focused on non-profit governance, offers *Board Basics 101: Board Orientation.*

Board Size, Board Processes, and Advisory Boards

Common answers you hear to the often-asked question of "What is an ideal board size is?" is "It depends on what your organization needs" or "What do you think it should be?"

Cornelis de Kluyver, dean of the University of Oregon's Lundquist College of Business, observed that the average Standard & Poor's (S&P's) 500 company's board of directors has 11 members.[9] He finds this is substantially lower than the average of 18 board members, which was the case 25 years ago. Clearly, despite the increasing complexity of the post–Sarbanes-Oxley corporate environment, for-profit corporation boards are tending to be relatively small, manageable groups, which generally conform to the studies of effective group decision making.

The BoardSource Nonprofit Governance Index 2010 indicates that the average for the hundreds of nonprofits in their study was 16 directors.[10] Recent NACD surveys show nonprofit boards averaging 17.9 directors, private companies averaging 7.3 directors, and public company boards averaging in size from 7.3 directors for what are called "nano-cap companies" to 12 directors for the "mega-cap companies."

Advisory boards are something you see a good bit in the nonprofit world for special purposes like fund-raising or building a capital campaign leadership team. You also see them with private companies that are not quite ready yet to add voting statutory directors to their board, but want the advice and counsel of a dedicated group of experts. Most public companies do not make heavy use of advisory boards. But they sometimes come into play when pharmaceutical or IT companies create advisory panels for their products.

Good practice for advisory boards includes clear written descriptions of their roles, responsibilities, and mandates. It is smart to distinguish their roles from the statutory or governing board for the organization. Likewise, never hesitate to place a sunset provision in an advisory board's mandate or disband the group when its work is done.

Board Charters

Many well-run companies have had charters, or committee policies and procedures, for many years to direct the work of their committees. Modern charters have their origins compliments of the U.S. Securities and Exchange Commission (SEC). The agency listed rules that were initially intended to improve audit committee effectiveness. Charters were later standardized by the Sarbanes-Oxley Act of 2002.

Today, written and published board charters of a more standardized nature are a mandatory requirement for the audit, compensation, and nominating and governance committees of public companies listed on the New York Stock Exchange (NYSE) and the Nasdaq Stock Market (NASDAQ). A board charter lays the foundation and provides a road map for great work by any committee.

Key elements of a good board committee charter include:

▸ Mission, purpose, and values
▸ Functions and duties

- Authority and responsibilities
- The size, skills, attributes, and experience desired for committee members
- The required or suggested frequency of committee meetings and the right to call special or private meetings with most or all parties of the company
- The right to periodically review and recommend to the board changes in the charter

Keep in mind, as well, that a good charter can directly or indirectly create legal and compliance obligations for the company, especially for a public company. In setting standards, a charter suggests promises of what will be accomplished. As you might expect, legal counsel normally is actively involved in the drafting and review of committee charters.

Charters may vary in length and content, based on the requirements of federal and state laws, listing standards of the company's stock exchange, and the needs of each company. Public company charters for the key audit, compensation, and nominating and governance committees are required to be published on company websites. That provides easy access to review and study charters from a wide range of companies of various sizes and industries. All public companies have their charters easily available under the Investor Relations sections of their websites.

CASE STUDY: NEW ERA FACES THE FUTURE

Jane Maddox settled into her seat on a plane bound for the New Era strategy retreat and anticipated the next two days of meetings. New

Era was Jane's first public company board, and while eager to both serve and learn from this opportunity, she needed to sort out what was so troubling about her New Era experience and what actions she might take at the meetings with the board. Were her concerns just part of the territory with a growing, highly entrepreneurial, young company . . . or another matter altogether?

New Era History

Cofounder John Fox began his career as a dedicated college professor at a struggling nonprofit college. Through hard work and a little luck, John acquired the college and made a modest go of it for several years. He joked that he was the last professor standing when the college went bankrupt.

John then connected with Jack Dempsey, a renowned venture capitalist known for success and risky ventures. They quickly hammered out a deal that included Dempsey's son coming on board "to make things happen," and happen they did. The growth was fast, culminating in a highly publicized, oversubscribed initial public offering (IPO).

Jane's History and Connection to New Era

Jane was a fast-track star performer with a mind for education. A top legal education and major law firm experience led to her role as dean of an up-and-coming law school, but a serious illness required her to leave the position for 2 years.

Once back on her feet, Jane took a leadership role with the U.S. Department of Education (DOE). Still, she was an entrepreneurial leader and dreamed of a college presidency. In a bit of luck, a friend named Sylvia Woods reached out to Jane about a board opportunity with New Era.

Jane did her due diligence and, in due course, was elected an independent director with New Era after she left the DOE. New Era had a tight group of directors, so Jane wisely received three assurances before joining the board: that other new independent directors were in the pipeline, she would have full access to senior management and information, and that quality teaching was a priority.

Jane's Actions over the Next Two Days of Strategy Retreat

Jane was skilled, savvy, and gracious, but major concerns were developing. In her two years of service, no new independent directors had been elected, the access to management and information she was promised was not coming, and a shocking report on outside probes was delivered from General Counsel Terry Howard, just as she headed for her flight to the retreat.

She used the plane ride to look over the report. What she read truly stunned her: investigations by the U.S. Department of Justice, the SEC, the U.S. Department of Education, and multiple state Attorneys General offices. There were probationary periods handed down from accrediting bodies. There were class-action lawsuits.

Jane's Concerns and Possible Actions:

1. **Jane's workload and the promised independent directors.**
   Jane expected 4 to 6 meetings a year, but had 22 meetings and 20 days of work in 10 months. She requested an executive

session of only outside directors to address the lack of new directors and other vital matters.

2. **Jane's struggle to work collaboratively with management while maintaining her clear independence as a board member.** Executive Vice President Julia Turner has formed a close bond with Jane. She relies heavily on Jane's contacts at the Department of Education, and sends Jane on visits to school sites and regulatory meetings across the country.

   Jane has little access to CEO Jack Dempsey and top executives except EVP Julia Turner and Founder John Fox, who is in failing health. Her calls to General Counsel Terry Howard are often ignored or provide few answers, until the shocking list of probes that she has just received.

   Jane sees no evidence of any serious executive performance evaluations, current succession planning, or active management development. She wonders if now is the time to surface these issues and who of those attending the retreat is willing to tackle them with her.

3. **Jane's genuine concern about the company's hard-sell pressure tactics.** Jane believes the company's hard-sell pressure tactics tarnish the quality and integrity of the academic product, as suggested by the many probes.

   A recent conversation with EVP of Sales Tom Dempsey highlights her concerns. He believes it's his model that makes this company work, and that regulatory matters can be resolved through fines, taxes, and professional fees. Dropout rates are high because New Era gives everyone a chance where others do not and students pay their own way. Positive satisfaction surveys from students prove his point, but Jane questions the ethics and legality of Tom's incentive-based model, especially when student loans are involved. Tom says incentives are essential to success—it is why they call it a sales force.

4. **Jane is concerned about the tangled web of related-party transactions.** She's heard through her network that Tom Dempsey, EVP of Sales and sales leader, has a major investment in, if not outright ownership control of, the primary outside vendor that New Era relies on for the majority of its student leads and direct mail advertising campaigns.

    Jane investigated corporate ownership for the company names she heard about, and it seems to be true. It appears other executives and directors have ownership as well.

    Jane remembers Sylvia Wood's concern that earnings and return on investment were slow coming. Jane acknowledges the amazing sales growth, but has never understood where the growth comes from or how it is attained. Should Jane discuss these matters with Sylvia and the board?

    It appears General Counsel Terry Howard's only client is Jack Dempsey and his many companies. Is Terry Howard functioning properly and successfully as general counsel to New Era and the board?

5. **Jane's concern about potential need for several key transitions in executive leadership.** It's apparent that President John Fox is no longer able to lead. Jane learned through private conversations with EVP Julia Turner that EVP of Sales Tom Dempsey wants to be president and CEO with plans to leave New Era for its primary competitor if not chosen. Does Jane

have a duty to share with the board the confidential plans of Tom Dempsey she learned of in private?

If EVP of Sales Tom Dempsey is nominated CEO, does Jane bring up his related party vendor relationship? Does his two-year associate degree disqualify him from the role of CEO?

6. **Jane's desire for an independent investigation by a board committee into the probes.** The General Counsel summary of New Era probes demands attention. Jane wants a board committee appointed for an independent investigation into the many probes. Is it the smart thing to do right now and what is the proper way to move forward? What if she is denied?

Next Steps

Jane's flight arrives and pulls up to the gate. Jane finds that Sylvia Woods e-mailed during the flight asking to talk before the strategy retreat. EVP of Sales Tom Dempsey also requested a meeting. Jane wonders what they might have in mind. The next two days will be critical for Jane.

Discussion Questions

1. What is Jane's first action after she gets off the plane?
2. How many independent directors were there on the board?
3. Did Jane do her due diligence? What more could she have done?
4. Was Jane working too hard and overinvolved with management?
5. Were there any shortcomings with Terry Howard as General Counsel?
6. Was Jane's experience unusual for a rapidly growing venture company?

7. What do you see as the top risk or concern for Jane and New Era?
8. Is it an independent director's job to take on a powerful CEO?
9. Does Jane have any leverage here? What is her leverage?
10. Has Jane made an impact on this company?
11. What do you think really happened?

New Era Follow-up: What Really Happened?

For the period 2004 through 2009, the for-profit college industry experienced intense scrutiny. This case represents *a compilation* of real events encountered by some of the top for-profit public companies and their colleges.

Did Jane make a bad call in joining the board of directors of the public company New Era?   *No. A small-cap board can face issues with family, friends, or a lack of independence and cronyism.*

Jane was eager to join her first public company board as an independent director. While there were structural red flags, she was careful with due diligence and received key assurances as a new director. She worked hard, made top contributions, and patiently learned the ropes. Her problem was not her decision to join; it was the conflict of good governance ideals versus the structure of a venture funded small-cap company. Few independent directors and cronyism were likely issues.

Good governance dialogue focuses on large corporations resulting in "one-size-fits-all" governance. Seven of ten U.S.-listed public companies have market caps of less than $500 million. In companies of this size large investors often call the shots and can influence board conduct. Independent directors can be stymied at every turn.[11]

What were the major issues regarding effective governance that Jane faced with New Era? *The executive team was weak, transparency and dialogue were missing, and core values were bad.*

The experience level of the executive team is inadequate considering the size, complexity, and growth of the company. General Counsel Terry Howard is likely conflicted, overwhelmed, or not up to his position. He consistently dodges or ignores Jane's phone calls. EVP of Sales Tom Dempsey's and EVP Julia Turner's relationships with Jane raise concerns of independence and confidentiality. These concerns also point to possible shortcomings in Julia's skill set, indicating the need for attention or support.

Jane was right to be concerned on the need for several key transitions in Executive Leadership. There is not a tradition of transparency, dialogue, or discussion between Jane and management despite her efforts. After two years, Jane has had little access to the Chair, CEO, or EVP.

The company pursued growth at any price, and, while Jane was amazed by the sales growth, she could not pinpoint where the sales came from, and was rightly concerned with the ethics of New Era's hard-sell pressure tactics.

What did Jane do that was right in serving on the New Era board of directors? *Jane did a great deal right in seeking progress with good governance for New Era.*

Jane's persistent demands produced the report on ongoing probes from the general counsel. Her request for an executive session of outside directors and her diligence in identifying the number of operating issues and ethical concerns on poor core values stoked the fire for change. Jane is ready to speak out at the coming board retreat and key directors are ready to listen.

What decisions or actions could Jane use as a director to immediately provoke results?   *There are many, including:*

- Meet with interested directors and have executive session of outside directors.
- Request the audit committee meet with the outside auditors on the probes.
- Inquire about the auditors and why the probes were not disclosed earlier.
- Request board committee or special counsel for independent review of probes.
- Request special counsel for review of related-party transactions and sales tools.
- Request special counsel to review whether New Era meets current independent director requirements for stock exchanges, higher education regulatory requirements, and more.

While the many shortcomings at New Era seem overwhelming, there was no indication of outright accounting or financial reporting fraud. Caution could dictate looking for accounting comfort from additional fraud-prevention tools, techniques, themes, and steps for strong accounting, like adding:

- Strong finance and accounting staff
- Strong internal auditor function
- Strong external audit function
- Robust whistleblower hotline processes
- Strong board audit committee
- Strong financial experts on board, including specialists in education

What best practices for excellence with boards and governance would help New Era? *Best practices for excellence with directors, boards, and governance overall would include:*

- Have capable independent directors.
- Have a thriving productive board culture.
- Have continuous governance evaluation and improvement.
- Provide effective oversight of CEO and organization performance.

In the End

After two years of heavy lifting, Jane's hard work and diligence finally paid off. She was elected to a second term, and helped New Era become a well-managed model of good corporate governance by executive turnover, remedied business practices, and growing profit margins.

Jane had some trouble with her first public company board service at New Era, but she paid her dues and learned valuable lessons. She now serves on two additional public company boards.[12]

Chapter 4

The Importance of Finance to Exemplary Directorship

A re you financially literate? You don't have to be an expert with numbers to join a board. But it's helpful. And the longer that you serve on a board, the more important financial literacy becomes as you deal with a welter of issues that come before you and your fellow directors.

Many support the view that every director would be well served to become financially literate. In boardrooms long ago, the audit committee was often the first committee assignment received by those new to board service, with the intent for the new director to learn the business of that company and industry, learn finance, and pay his or her dues. New board members typically emerged from several years of audit committee service with strong financial literacy, good working knowledge of the company's operations, and a broad understanding of the industry it operated in.

Financial literacy simply means board members have a basic ability to understand the finances and financial statements of the company they serve. Can they understand the financial presentations made to them by management about the company and industry? Can they have meaningful discussions with the company's controller or chief financial officer (CFO) and external auditors when financial matters are discussed? Can they grasp basic financial transactions described to them by commercial bankers, investment bankers, insurance agents and the like? Can they follow the flow of funds through a business from the point of sale until it reaches the bottom line?

In recent years, changes brought on by the Sarbanes-Oxley Act of 2002 and the Dodd-Frank Act of 2010 resulted in a targeted approach enforced through the public market stock exchanges where each public company board is required to have a designated independent financial expert.

Each company is required to identify their financial expert in their public reports. Financial expertise is a high standard far beyond the concept of having basic financial literacy.

In my many years of working with boards and in governance, I have only discovered one organization that enforces a specific financial skills requirement for all directors. The National Credit Union Administration (NCUA) in 2011 issued a NCUA final rule, Regulation §701.4 called "General authorities and duties of Federal credit union directors." Their provision of the rule states: "A director must have at least a working familiarity with basic finance and accounting practices, including the ability to read and understand the Federal credit union's balance sheet and income statement and the ability to ask, as appropriate, substantive questions of management and the internal and external auditors." See Figure 4.1 for a

FIGURE 4.1 Is Financial Literacy a Prerequisite for a Good Director?

An "●" in the chart below indicates that the item is a specific reason that the director has been nominated to serve on the company's board.

NOMINEES FOR THE BOARD*

	1	2	3	4	5	6	7	8	9	10	11	12	13	14
High level of financial literacy	●	●		●				●		●		●	●	●
Diversity of race, ethnicity, age, gender, cultural background or professional experience			●		●	●		●	●				●	
Extensive knowledge of the company's business, industry, or manufacturing	●	●			●	●		●			●	●		●
Marketing/marketing-related technology experience	●		●	●		●	●				●	●	●	
Broad international exposure or specific in-depth knowledge of a key geographic growth area		●	●	●	●		●	●		●			●	
Relevant Chief Executive Officer/President experience		●	●	●		●	●	●			●			●
Governmental, political, or diplomatic expertise				●				●	●	●		●		

A look at a company's shareholder report can reveal what qualities a board values in its search. This theoretical pool of nominees shows that nearly half of the nominees did not have a high level of financial literacy when under consideration. However, once a director gets on a board, he or she can grow his or her financial skills.

*The lack of a dot for a particular qualification does not mean that the director does not possess that qualification or skill. Rather, a dot indicates a specific area of focus or expertise of a director on which the board currently relies.

Source: Tom Bakewell

comparison of different qualities of directors with the importance of financial literacy.

Any new director joining a Federal credit union board today has six months to gain the requisite financial skills. Interestingly, the regulators tie this financial literacy and skills requirement directly to risk as a component of the directors' duties in stating: "To do their job in a meaningful manner, it is essential that directors understand the risks found in depository institutions—that is, credit, liquidity, interest rate, compliance, strategic, transaction, and reputation risk. Moreover, directors must understand the internal control structures at the credit union that limit and control those risks." This statement highlights the value of this chapter on the importance of finance to exemplary directorship.

For a simple measuring stick, use three standards of financial literacy, including:

▶ Little or no financial literacy
▶ Good or growing financial literacy
▶ Near or qualified as a financial expert

Don't be fearful of accepting a board seat for lack of financial literacy. Do accept the challenge to get better at it.

If you are serious about growing your level of financial literacy there are a hundred ways. Here are a few tips to consider.

Take a crash course in accounting. *Accounting* is the language of business. Few directors would have the time to retool by taking entry- or advanced-level accounting and finance classes, but there are many bar associations, accounting firms, and universities that offer superb short programs on key financial topics like finance for directors, financial statement review, and financial analysis.

The major accounting firms have regular programs focused exclusively on audit committee matters. KPMG has a well-known Audit Committee Institute (ACI). Also, all of the larger accounting firms actively publish on auditing and audit committees. Generally, these are available on request at little or no cost.

Take your favorite certified public accountant (CPA), controller, or chief financial officer (CFO) to lunch and have him or her carefully walk you through a full set of financial statements or a financial report you can't decipher. And, if you are on a board, have a serious conversation with the board chair about joining the audit committee and getting a tutorial from the audit committee chair or company finance executive. If the board is for a public company, find out if there are any reports by outside analysts or calls by analysts. Review the reports and listen to the calls. Commit the time and you will grow your financial literacy.

AUDITS

Every board member will face the challenge of dealing with audits. Audits can refer widely to any number of external or internal evaluations performed for a company with the goal of expressing some type of expert opinion on a particular matter. Examples of audits in the corporate world include: audits involving financial statements, IRS tax audits, compliance audits, personnel audits, employee benefit audits, operating audits, and information technology audits. Typical audit steps include:

- ▶ Preparing an audit work plan.
- ▶ Reviewing the planned audit process with the leadership involved.
- ▶ Discussing with management a draft of the key findings.
- ▶ Completing the audit report for release to leadership.
- ▶ Issuing the final report and following up, as needed.

Financial statement audits refer more specifically to an external examination of a company's books, records, and related disclosures by an independent auditor. The auditor will express some type of opinion attesting that the financial statements and disclosures as prepared by the company are fairly presented. The financial statement audit is typically used by a company to provide a wide range of company stakeholders (like bankers, customers, suppliers, employees, investors, and owners) with a respected level of independent assurance and comfort that the financial statements fairly represent the company's financial position and performance. Auditors are typically qualified member accountants of a professional accounting association in their respective country like Certified Public Accountants in the United States or Chartered Accountants in the United Kingdom.

Auditors are ultimately selected by shareholders and typically report to them through the company audit committee of the board of directors. Companies of all sizes and ownership structures prepare financial statements and many voluntarily elect to have audits performed. Companies listed on the public company stock exchanges are required to have annual independent audits. The external auditors of all publicly traded companies are subject to the stringent audit committee requirements of the Public Company Accounting Oversight Board (PCAOB), a creation of the Sarbanes-Oxley Act of 2002.

Most private companies of any material size in the United States have annual independent audits performed to facilitate ongoing operations with bankers, suppliers, and customers. Most nonprofits in the United States have annual independent audits performed to comply with Internal Revenue Service (IRS) requirements in filing the annual Form 990, Return of Organization Exempt from Income Tax to maintain their tax-exempt status and as a matter of good governance.

Company management is responsible for preparing financial statements. The auditor is responsible for expressing an opinion, giving some reasonable assurance that the financial statements when taken as a whole are free from material misstatement and are fairly presented according to relevant accounting standards.

Let me say that again. *Company management is responsible for preparing financial statements, not the auditors.* Figure 4.2 clearly reflects this relationship.

Public company reports that are published, like the Form 10-K, will have specific disclosures along with the independent auditors' reports emphasizing three key relationships and responsibilities:

1. **Report of Management.** It clearly states, in detail, that management is responsible for the preparation and integrity of company financial statements.

2. **Management's Report on Internal Control over Financial Reporting Management of the Company.** It states that management is responsible for establishing and maintaining adequate internal control over financial reporting as is defined in Rule 13a-15(f) under the Securities Exchange Act of 1934.

3. **Audit Committee, composed solely of Directors.** The audit committee is independent in accordance with the requirements of the stock exchange listing standards, the Exchange Act, and the Company's Corporate Governance Guidelines, and meets with the independent auditors.

FIGURE 4.2 Who's Responsible for a Financial Statement?

REPORT OF MANAGEMENT

"Management of the company is responsible for the preparation and integrity of the consolidated financial statements appearing in our annual report on Form 10-K."

The Audit Committee is "composed solely of directors who are **independent**, in accordance with the requirements of the New York Stock Exchange listing standards. . . ."

ACCOUNTING FIRM DISCLAIMER:

"Management is responsible for maintaining effective internal control over financial reporting."

CONTROLS AND PROCEDURES:

"The Company, under the supervision and with the participation of its management, including the **Chief Executive Officer** and the **Chief Financial Officer**, evaluate the effectiveness of the design and operation of the Company's 'disclosure controls and procedures.'"

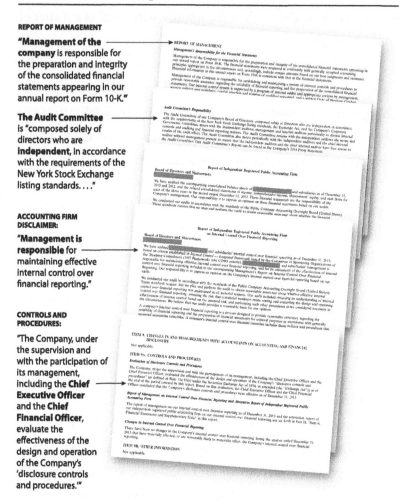

A look at one company's annual report shows that management is ultimately responsible for the accurate reporting of a company's finances—not the accounting firm.

An audit opinion will be clearly stated as a separate carefully worded paragraph found in the audit report. The auditor gives a *clean or unqualified audit opinion* where it concludes that the company's financial statements are free from material misstatement. If an auditor cannot issue a clean or *unqualified audit opinion*, the company may have real challenges on its hands.

Beyond clean audit opinions, there are a handful of alternate modified audit opinions including a *qualified audit opinion*, a *disclaimer of opinion*, and an *adverse opinion*. Modified opinions can indicate a disagreement with management that is unresolved, an inability by the auditor to perform the work it deemed necessary, or an inability by the auditor to gather the evidence it needs. Auditors can highlight a particular concern by emphasizing that matter in their audit reports. An adverse opinion implies company financial statements are deemed unreliable by the auditor.

A *going-concern opinion* is an unqualified audit opinion that has language expressing concern about the company's ability to continue to operate as a viable going concern. When reviewing an auditor opinion letter, take special note of the parties the letter is addressed to and the specific dates of the letter.

Evaluating Internal Controls

As we move into the topic of internal controls be aware that we are now entering an area that goes way beyond basic financial literacy and into the zone of financial expertise. Do not be intimidated in reviewing the concepts. The basic concepts of internal controls are fairly simple. The application of them can be complex. To review the topic of internal controls we will highlight in italics a few key terms.

Internal controls, according to one common definition, are "methods put in place by a company to ensure the integrity of financial and accounting information, meet operational and profitability targets and transmit management policies throughout the organization."[1]

Many of the key concepts of good internal control include common accounting and management practices widely used by many today. But every organization is free to develop its own financial and accounting systems along with its own approaches to internal control.

Generally, *internal control processes* are determined by management with oversight by the board. The board, through its audit committee, can have an important role in setting the standards for the company to have good internal controls. But finding the right level of control, in the right places in the company, can be a tricky balancing act requiring great skill. Rigid control can be costly and slow business operations. A low level of control can result in bad practices, fraud, theft, and waste. Many of the best internal control tools have always been the simplest: the segregation of duties among multiple employees, multiple approvals, mandatory reconciliation of accounts, strong security over pricey assets, required extended vacations for company officers controlling financial matters, and robust audit programs.

Internal Control over Financial Reporting (ICFR) relates to the basic concept of attempting to determine if an organization's internal controls are doing the job and resulting in good and accurate financial reporting. Section 404(b) of the Sarbanes-Oxley Act (SOX) of 2002 requires that an independent auditor attest to management's assessment of the effectiveness of those internal controls. Therefore, an organization must perform financial reporting contingent upon its internal controls. In public companies, the management team is required to assess and report on the effectiveness of the internal controls over financial reporting. Independent external auditors are then required, as part of their audits, to attest that management's assessments of internal control are effective.

An *internal audit* is an internal review process and function that companies are wise to adopt once they reach any substantial size and can afford the investment. The idea is to have skilled team members who spend their time independently confirming that the company's many activities, policies, and procedures are being applied in the proper way. Opportunities for improvement can sometimes be found. Independent review ensures that the management team is regularly working in the best interest of the owners and not over-reaching with actions for their personal benefit. As part of any audit, there is always the need to have an eye and ear open to the risks of fraud, theft, and misuse of company assets.

Public companies are required under Sarbanes-Oxley to have an internal audit function. There are also listing requirements of common stock exchanges that audit committees will periodically meet separately with internal audit leadership. Internal audit is a function that can be developed in-house, but many companies elect to contract the function to outside organizations that specialize full-time in internal auditing. Most large organizations have an executive responsible for internal audits. There are many resources available to internal auditors like the Institute of Internal Auditors (IIA).

External audit refers to the process of overseeing the work of an outside independent accountant who performs an audit of the company's financial statements and express an opinion. One of the regular responsibilities of most boards and directors is to oversee the preparation, performance, and completion of the independent external audit. A great external audit process and report can go a long way toward a board satisfying its general and fiduciary obligations as directors.

Boards typically have an audit committee that takes the lead in selecting, engaging, and working with the accounting firm they want to handle the external audit. Public companies today on the major stock exchanges are required to have audit committees comprised *only* of independent directors. They have the direct power to select, negotiate with, and terminate the company auditors, with shareholders normally ratifying the auditor selection at the annual meeting.

Material misstatements in financial records are the bane of every auditor, company, and shareholder. Good internal controls are one of the top tools to prevent or catch financial fraud and the other matters that can result in the need for a company to publish a *restatement* of its previously issued financial statements. Class-action lawsuits against companies and boards by shareholders often follow immediately after a company announces any material misstatement of its financial records or a restatement of its financial statements. Figure 4.3 gives a vivid picture of the annual number of restatements for public companies from 2001 to 2012 and tells the story that even large public companies with the resources to have talented accountants and auditors can face financial reporting challenges resulting in restatements.

FIGURE 4.3 Total Restatement by Large U.S. Companies

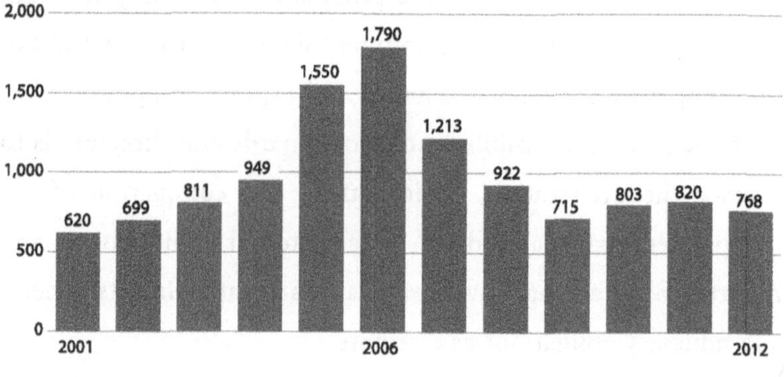

Source: Audit Analytics

Examples of the Failure of Internal Controls

As a wrap to our section on internal controls, let's look at two recent situations that highlight the failure of internal controls. Both led to major financial losses.

The basic risk of fraud is always present. In 1973 Dr. Donald Cressey created a fraud triangle to explain how a normally trustworthy employee steals (see Figure 4.4).[2]

Rita Crundwell served as chief financial officer (CFO) for the city of Dixon, Illinois, for decades. She made a modest salary managing an annual city budget in the $8 to $10-million range. Crundwell also lived large as one of the top owners of champion horses in the luxury world of quarter horses. In April 2012, Crundwell was fired for alleged embezzlement of some $30 million from city coffers.[3] In 2013, Crundwell was sentenced to 235 months in prison for stealing almost $54 million.[4] Subsequent settlements were made with Dixon's external auditor for some $35 million, with Dixon's internal auditor for $1 million, and with a bank for almost $4 million.[5]

FIGURE 4.4 The Fraud Triangle

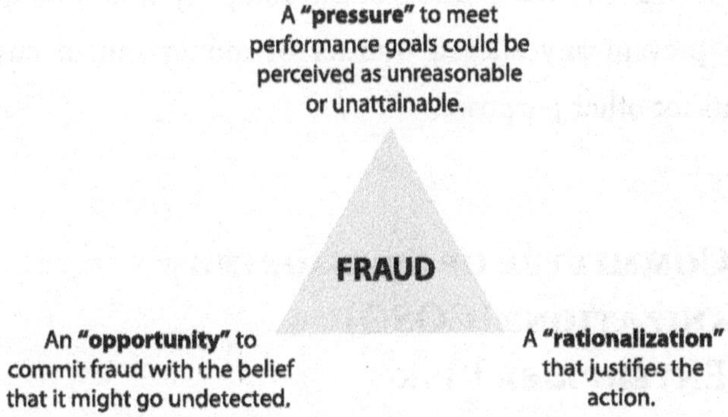

A **"pressure"** to meet
performance goals could be
perceived as unreasonable
or unattainable.

FRAUD

An **"opportunity"** to
commit fraud with the belief
that it might go undetected.

A **"rationalization"**
that justifies the
action.

Three conditions are usually present when fraud occurs. Boards should take care to make sure their company culture is not conducive to fraud.

At least part of the damage may have been caused by a major internal control failure. Crundwell had created huge capital construction accounts to cover the missing funds for major projects that were never approved and never existed. The auditors apparently never checked to see if these major projects existed. They didn't exist. A fairly standard audit test is to visit job sites and look at physical assets like buildings under construction or recently completed. Other shortcomings were alleged in the audits as well.

MF Global Holdings Ltd. was a large commodity futures broker headed by CEO Jon S. Corzine, a former New Jersey governor. MF Global collapsed and filed for bankruptcy protection in October 2011.[6] The U.S. Commodity Futures Trading Commission (CFTC) filed a suit accusing Corzine and assistant treasurer Edith O'Brien of illegally transferring money out of customer accounts to stem losses from other trading by the company.[7] At the time, federal laws required futures brokers to keep customer funds separate and barred them from using funds elsewhere. Shareholders also accused PricewaterhouseCoopers (PwC) of professional negligence, although the court eventually dismissed all claims against PwC.[8] Strong internal controls at the company would be the best tool to prevent any alleged transfer of money out of customer accounts for other purposes.

THE COMMITTEE OF SPONSORING ORGANIZATIONS (COSO) AND ENTERPRISE RISK

Maintaining internal control requires human attention, devotion to process, and a willingness to adapt to changing times and changing requirements. An organization known as "COSO" addresses many of these issues.

COSO, The Committee of Sponsoring Organizations of the Treadway Commission, is the product of five private U.S. organizations: the American Accounting Association (AAA), the American Institute of Certified Public Accountants (AICPA), the Financial Executives International (FEI), The Institute of Internal Auditors (IIA) and the Institute of Management Accountants (IMA).[9] In 1992, these groups created the Internal Control–Integrated Framework.[10] The COSO Framework was updated in 2013 to stay abreast of changing business models, increased business risk, emerging technologies, global integration, and higher shareholder expectations. The COSO Framework aids other companies and organizations trying to stay in compliance with the Sarbanes-Oxley Act of 2002, Section 404, and the Securities Exchange Act of 1934.

According to the COSO Framework, internal control is a process executed by the board of directors or managerial staff to provide reasonable assurance in the areas of efficiency, financial reporting, regulatory compliance, and safeguarding assets. Five COSO Framework components are emphasized in the COSO documents, and reflected on the COSO cube shown in Figure 4.5.[11]

1. *Control environments.* First, a control environment is a necessary foundation for internal control. The proper environment sets the tone of the organization and establishes precedents for ethics, integrity, operating style, and delegation.[12]
2. *Risk assessment.* Second, risk assessment is vital to managing both external and internal risk. The COSO Framework

FIGURE 4.5 The COSO Cube

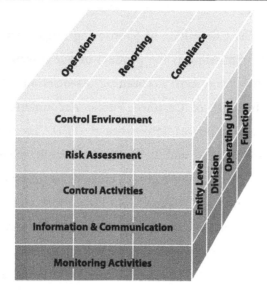

Reprinted by permission of the Committee of Sponsoring Organizations of the Treadway Commission (COSO), 2013.

presents strategies for establishing objectives and assigning them, so that companies may confront risk as it arises.

3. *Control activities.* Third, the COSO Framework guides management by describing "control activities," or the procedures and policies to assist approvals, authorizations, verifications, reconciliations, reviews of operating performance, security of assets, and segregation of duties as well as others.

4. *Information and communication.* Fourth, establishing systems of information and communication is vital to producing reports and organizing compliance-related information. Communication is a priority in any organization, but established and effective communication helps prevent slowdown, the need for corrective actions, and even fraud.

5. *Monitoring.* Fifth, COSO addresses the monitoring of internal
   control systems and maintaining system quality over time.
   This requires constant evaluation so that deficiencies may be
   addressed and improvements made.

The process of internal control integration is not an item to be
completed. It's a goal-based system that constantly changes as each
organization grows and the global business evolves. Board members,
an audit committee, or a specified risk-management committee should
constantly reaffirm their company's compliance practices. Enterprise risk management depends on human judgment, so mistakes
and errors are inevitable. This is why the COSO Framework calls
for "reasonable assurance" as opposed to "absolute assurance," and
emphasizes a strong internal control system.

COSO addressed enterprise risk management framework in a
2001 project in cooperation with PricewaterhouseCoopers. At that
time, scandals and failures were exposed in several high-profile
businesses such as Enron Corporation, Tyco International, World-
Com, and others. The collaboration produced the *Enterprise Risk
Management–Integrated Framework*, a document intended to sup-
plement the *Internal Control–Integrated Framework*, in 2004. This
new document focused specifically on risk management, using strategic high-level goals, effective and efficient use of resources, reliable reporting, and regulatory compliance.

The COSO *Internal Control-Integrated Framework*—and its
companion document, the *Enterprise Risk Management–Integrated
Framework*—is only one framework model used to meet Sarbanes-
Oxley, Section 404 compliance goals. Other frameworks available
include COBIT® (from ISACA), Auditing Standard No. 2 (from

PCAOB), and SAS 55/78 (from AICPA), although, according to a poll by *CFO Magazine* in March 2006, 82 percent of respondents used the COSO framework.[13]

OVERVIEW OF FINANCIAL STATEMENTS

The basic financial statements are the Income Statement, Balance Sheet, Statement of Stockholders' Equity, and Statement of Cash Flows.

The *Income Statement* measures a company's financial performance over a specific period of time. For example, a typical Annual Income Statement can be for a calendar year like 2013. Income statements can be for any period of time like monthly, quarterly, or something specific like the "Fiscal Year Ending September 30, 2013."

The *Balance Sheet* presents a company's financial position as of a specified date and generally includes assets, liabilities, and equity. It is also known as a "Statement of Financial Position." The Balance Sheet gives a snapshot or picture of overall financial position at a specified moment in time.

The *Statement of Stockholders' Equity* refers to the ownership interest held in a company. Alternate names include equity, net worth, or fund balance. Typical items found in equity include paid-in or contributed capital, common stock, preferred stock, and retained earnings.

The *Statement of Cash Flows* tracks the cash flows in and out of a company. This statement shows, for a period of time, how the changes from the operations of the business and the related income, for a period of time, impact the Balance Sheet accounts. Cash and positive cash flows are vital to the operations of a business, and the

Statement of Cash Flows helps provide a clear picture on the ability of a business to have cash to pay its obligations.

The Balance Sheet, the Income Statement, and the Statement of Cash Flows typically interact and are connected with a starting Balance Sheet at a point in time, followed by an Income Statement and a Statement of Cash Flows for a period in time the company operated, connected to an ending Balance Sheet. Visually this is reflected as follows:

TABLE 4.1 Connection of the Balance Sheet, the Income Statement, and the Statement of Cash Flows

	Income Statement 2013 Period of Time	
Starting Balance Sheet 2012 Year End Point in Time e.g., 12/31/2012	⟶ e.g., 1/1/2013 through 12/31/2013	**Ending Balance Sheet** 2013 Year End Point in Time e.g., 12/31/2013
	Statement of Cash Flows for 2013 Period of Time	

Companies, especially public companies, often prepare an Annual Report. Typically, this includes two groups of information; non-audited information and audited information. *Nonaudited information* includes items like letters or reports to owners or shareholders, a description of operations and activities, and a more formal management discussion and analysis commonly known as the MD&A. *Audited information* includes all the basic financial statements, the auditor's opinion letter, audit footnotes, and any statements of management's responsibility for the financial statements. When you receive an Annual Report, begin with the auditor's opinion. He or she will attest to the accuracy of the information and seek to give a clean, *unqualified audit opinion*. If unable to give a clean, unqualified audit opinion then you are likely to receive a *qualified audit opinion* (you will see the language "except for"). This is a red flag, and the statements should be examined skeptically. Perhaps, the results are properly stated and simply indicate the adoption of a new and required accounting standard, but again they may be misleading, incomplete, or inaccurate, and demand skepticism. What has the auditor questioned? Is there a *going-concern audit opinion* (concern about the company's ability to remain viable)? Is there a question of the method used for revenue recognition? These, and other significant matters, will be examined in this chapter.

FORM 10-K, MD&A, CD&A, FORM 8-K, ANNUAL REPORT, AND KEY FINANCIAL RATIOS

Related to financial statements and public companies, there are a handful of basic Securities and Exchange Commission (SEC) filings required including a proxy, Form 10-K, Form 10-Q, Form 8-K, and Form S-1. A *proxy* is a communication to shareholders regarding matters requiring shareholder action. *Form 10-K* is an annual report to the SEC that includes company financial statements and other disclosures. *Form 10-Q* is a quarterly report to the SEC. *Form 8-K* is a special report disclosing key activities such as a major acquisition, resignation of a director, or a change of auditors. *Form S-1* is a basic form to file for the registration of new issues of securities.

Several of these forms are covered here in greater detail.

Form 10-K

The government requires public companies to make disclosures that give investors a fair and accurate picture of financial health. The companies must file Form 10-K, a form that goes to the SEC and provides details about their financials, their goals and the risks they face.

Public companies also provide Annual Reports to their shareholders. They contain a lot of the same information as the 10-K, but in generally less detail and are typically packaged a bit more like glossy marketing material.

There are disclosures that must be in Form 10-K and companies cannot make false or misleading statements in completing the form. To help ensure that the disclosures are honest and accurate, Sarbanes-Oxley requires that a submitting company's chief executive officer (CEO) and chief financial officer (CFO) sign *certifications related* to the information in the 10-K. The SEC monitors Form 10-K disclosures and is required by Sarbanes-Oxley to review every public company's Form 10-K at least once every three years.

Form 10-Ks are available using the SEC's EDGAR (Electronic Data Gathering, Analysis, and Retrieval system), website, https://www.edgarfiling.sec.gov/, which receives and generally makes available to the public most documents that public companies file with the SEC. Companies often post their Form 10-Ks on their websites. Companies also must provide a copy of their Form 10-K to requesting shareholders.

In addition to Form 10-K, public companies must file Form 10-Q. This form is similar to Form 10-K except that it is far less detailed and must be filed with the SEC every quarter.

Form 8-K, discussed below, is a way to update Form 10-K. The SEC requires that material events, e.g., a bankruptcy or a change in the CEO, be disclosed. Form 8-K provides a vehicle for such disclosure.

Sections of Form 10-K

Part I

Part I includes a description of the company's business—what the company does to make money. Part I also includes risk factors for the company, its reaction to SEC questions about the company's operations, the companies physical footprint, including its buildings and properties, and finally any significant legal proceedings affecting the company.

Risk factors could be particularly interesting to investors. These may be fairly basic, including the volatility of the stock market and the possibility of another economic downturn. Investors should look out for risk factors particular to the company. Examples include large percentages of the company's profits coming from a few clients or customers or a recent multitude of lawsuits against the company.

Part II

While Part I contains what is essentially a basic introduction to the company, Part II includes more in-depth financial information vital to investors. There is a multiyear summary of revenues, profits, assets, and debts, and a look at the possible effects of market turbulence on the company's assets.

Most important, perhaps, is the section containing the management's discussion and analysis of the company's performance. Here, the company's executives give their own explanations of how the company is doing and why it is performing that way.

Part II also includes any disagreements or changes the company has with its auditors. Conflicts with auditors may be indicative of untrustworthy numbers.

Part III

Part III is focused on the individuals who run the company. Directors and officers are identified and their annual compensation is listed. The amount of shares owned by directors, officers, and major shareholders is listed, and director independence and possible conflict of interest disclosures are made, including those regarding the firm's accountants.

Part IV

Part IV contains corporate documents. Included are the company's articles of incorporation, bylaws, and important contracts.

Management's Discussion and Analysis

Part II of Form 10-K contains a section titled: Item 7. Management's Discussion and Analysis of Financial Condition and Results of Operations (MD&A). There must also be an MD&A section in a public company's Annual Report.

This MD&A section allows company leaders to discuss recent profits or losses and issues that may not be reflected in the company's financial statements. It also gives current or prospective investors a rare glimpse into a firm's management and management style.

The MD&A is intended to include a fair and complete analysis—looking through the lens of the company's executives and management—of how the firm has performed in the past, how it is performing currently, and how it is likely to perform in the future. Management will generally include a description of the coming year's goals and major projects.

Deciding what to include in the MD&A section is not easy. The SEC provides some guidance in completing the section, but the guidelines are general. The SEC requires that management merely "describe," "discuss," or "identify" certain aspects of the company, such as liquidity of assets, capital resources, unusual events such as mergers and acquisitions, and relevant trends or uncertainties.[14]

One expert has provided nine tips, summarized here, for companies completing the MD&A section of Form 10-K:[15]

1. Use plain language and helpful visual tools.
2. Use a *short* overview.
3. Employ a top-down analysis, discussing the most pressing issues first.
4. Pay attention to the disclosures of competitors because your disclosures will be compared to theirs.
5. State *why* the company is doing what it is doing or thinking what it is thinking.
6. Do not use generic, restated risk factors.
7. Use numbers when explaining the company's performance and how much the company was affected by the year's events.
8. Do not use separate charts for this year and last year; combine the information into one chart.
9. Have the company's disclosure committee watch for issues that may eventually need to be disclosed.

Compensation Discussion and Analysis

In 2006, the SEC dramatically expanded requirements for public companies to disclose executive compensation and compensation policies. Because of the rule change, companies are now required to include a "Compensation Discussion and Analysis" (CD&A) section in certain SEC filings.[16]

Similar to the required MD&A section, the CD&A section should provide a narrative explanation of the subject from the company leaders' points of view. The CD&A is intended to explain all material factors that go into the company's executives' and directors' compensation, and the company's compensation policies. Implementation of the decisions must be shown in a "Summary Compensation Table," among other tables.

Specifically, the CD&A must include:

▶ The objectives behind the company's compensation policies
▶ Each component of compensation (salary, bonus, equity, perks, etc.)
▶ The purpose for these components
▶ How the company determines the amount for each component
▶ How each compensation component fits into the company's overall compensation objectives
▶ The activities and values the compensation program is designed to reward.[17]

The CD&A should be written in plain English and not be made up of boilerplate.

The SEC has provided a list of examples of items that may be appropriate for the CD&A section:

▶ Policies for allocating between long-term and currently paid out compensation

- Policies for allocating between cash and noncash compensation, and among different forms of noncash compensation
- The factors considered in decisions to increase or decrease compensation materially
- The impact of accounting and tax treatments of a particular form of compensation
- Whether the company engaged in any benchmarking of total compensation or any material element of compensation, identifying the benchmark and, if applicable, its components (including component companies)
- The role of executive officers in the compensation process[18]

Form 8-K

Form 8-K is the "current report" companies must file with the SEC to announce major events that shareholders should know about. The instructions for Form 8-K describe the types of events that trigger a public company's obligation to file a current report, including any of the following:

- Section 1. Registrant's Business and Operations
- Section 2. Financial Information
- Section 3. Securities and Trading Markets
- Section 4. Matters Related to Accountants and Financial Statements
- Section 5. Corporate Governance and Management
- Section 6. Asset-Backed Securities (ABS)
- Section 7. Regulation Fair Disclosure (FD)
- Section 8. Other Events

You can find a company's Form 8-K filings on the SEC's EDGAR database.

Annual Report

There are certain sections typically included in an Annual Report. They are:

- ▶ Management's Discussion and Analysis (MD&A)
- ▶ Report of Independent Accountants. The primary matter to be observed in this document is the issuance of an "unqualified opinion."
- ▶ Footnotes to the Financial Statements
- ▶ Historical summary of results
- ▶ Company contact information

Key Financial Ratios

Financial analysis can be greatly enhanced by *financial ratios*. There are generally five types of recognized ratios:

1. **Liquidity.** Measures the firm's ability to pay debts and ongoing expenses as they mature.
2. **Leverage.** Measures the company's previous sources of resources (borrowings and invested capital).
3. **Activity.** Measures the frequency of movement of items, such as accounts receivable and inventory.
4. **Profitability.** Measures the percent of earnings against factors, such as sales or stockholder's equity.
5. **Other.** This is a category for ratios that do not fall into one of the preceding four types.

FIGURE 4.6 How to Read a Financial Statement in Plain English[19]

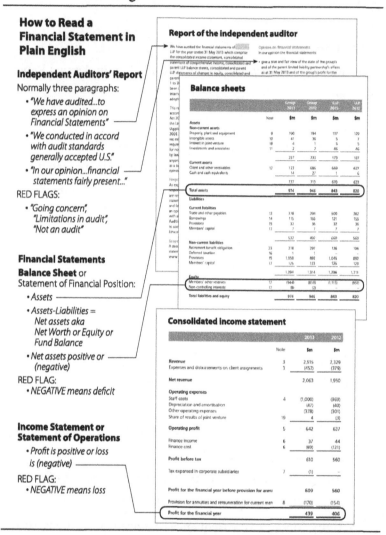

Ratios are difficult to evaluate in the absence of comparable metrics. Comparables can be secured in several different ways. Historical trend analysis can be enormously helpful. For example, how does this year's return on sales (ROS) compare to the past four years? Trend information can be very enlightening.

FIGURE 4.6 (Continued)

Statement of Changes in Equity
- Summary for the year (or period)
- Normally very simple
RED FLAG:
- NEGATIVE means deficit

Statement of Cash Flows

- Net cash flows from operating activities
- Net cash flows (used in) investing activities
- Net cash flows (used in) financing activities
- Net increase (decrease) in cash and cash equivalents
- Cash and cash equivalents, start of year, end of year
RED FLAGS:
- NEGATIVE cash flow from operating activities
- DECREASING OR NEGATIVE end-of-year cash

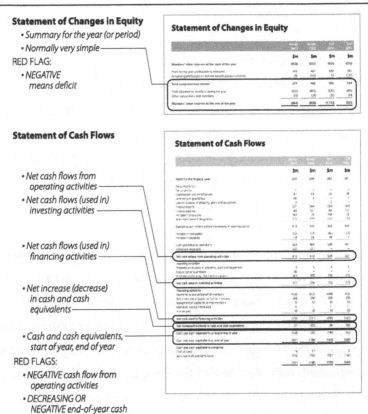

Source: Example of Generally Accepted Auditing Standards as applied to sample financial statements by Tom Bakewell, CPA.

THE NUMBERS DON'T LIE

Good accountants will tell you that the numbers don't lie. But what about a CEO, CFO, or executive team with intense pressure to make the numbers to keep their jobs or make a huge bonus? It is the board's job to create an environment where board members have confidence in the numbers, monitor performance of the company with a high degree of trust and skepticism, and regularly challenge and question both accounting practices and operating results.

At the most basic level, company finances can be grasped with really simple questions:

- ► How does this company make money?
- ► What is our business model and is it working?
- ► Do we have real and growing earnings from operations?
- ► Are our earnings from real operating profits or creative financial moves, like selling a building or liquidating other assets?
- ► Do we have positive cash flow from operations or are we living on a line of credit or our net worth?

While company finances can be simple to grasp on a macro basis, the details of sophisticated financial literacy can take years to learn. By way of example, a financially literate director will fully understand topics like asymmetrical information, mark-to-market accounting, the Foreign Corrupt Practices Act, cooking the books, and whistleblowers. Any one of these topics, and many more, can have a dramatic impact on a company and its finances.

Let's wrap our sections on the importance of finance with just a few more stories involving some of these topics and their impact on company finances. The intent is not to dissuade you from becoming financially literate, but rather to give you a final reality check on finance, human nature, and the major responsibility of not being naïve when it comes to financial reporting.

Foreign Corrupt Practices Act of 1977

Government corruption and bribery, particularly in developing countries, is problematic for corporations from a legal and operations standpoint, especially as regulations intensify. In the 1970s, the SEC investigated hundreds of American companies that eventually admitted to making hundreds of millions of dollars in payments to government officials, politicians, and political parties in exchange for business favors. In response to these scandals, President Jimmy Carter signed the Foreign Corrupt Practices Act (FCPA) into law on December 19, 1977.

The FCPA, which is enforced jointly by the U.S. Department of Justice (DOJ) and the U.S. Securities and Exchange Commission (SEC), was enacted to bolster the fight against corruption using official investigations and penalties, and works, in addition to laws barring racketeering, money laundering, and conspiracy. Corporate directors and managers of international companies must know the FCPA well so that they can understand when a situation involving possible corrupt practices arises and how to avoid a violation.

The FCPA bars not only bribery of foreign officials, but also accounting practices that attempt to hide bribery. Covered individuals and entities under the FCPA include those with formal ties to the United States and those who further violations of the FCPA while in the United States. Included in these classes are public companies in the United States, companies big and small headquartered in the United States, and residents of the United States.

An FCPA violation consists of the following elements:

1. A payment, offer, authorization, or promise to pay money or anything of value to a foreign government official (including a party official or manager of a state-owned concern), or to any other person, knowing that the payment or promise will be passed on to a foreign official

2. An individual or entity with a corrupt motive for the
   purpose of (a) influencing any act or decision of that person,
   (b) inducing such person to do or omit any action in violation
   of his lawful duty, (c) securing an improper advantage, or
   (d) inducing such person to use his influence to affect an
   official act or decision
3. In order to assist in obtaining or retaining business for or with,
   or directing any business to, any person[20]

Although the FCPA generally bars "knowing" violations, willful
blindness to the regulations will not be tolerated.[21]

Cooking the Books

A company's financial records or "books" can be incorrect either
through mistake or, more notably, through intentional alteration or
manipulation. "Cooking the books" or "creative accounting" typically
involves following generally accepted accounting principles (GAAP)
but deviating from the *spirit* of the rules. Incentives for doing this
include ensuring job security, covering up fraud, and buying time
with hopes of a business turnaround.

Some good examples of cooking the books or creative accounting include:

► **Bernie Madoff.** The embellishment by Bernie Madoff and
  his staff of financial data to show earnings that did not exist,
  actions which led to the defrauding of investors out of
  $60 billion (and a 150-year prison sentence for Madoff).[22]
► **Dewey & LeBoeuf LLP.** The now defunct, but once enormous,
  law firm Dewey & LeBoeuf allegedly used a variety of accounting

gimmicks to paint a misleading picture of its financial health, including requesting backdated checks from clients and classifying long-uncollectable bills as receivables.[23]

▶ **Olympus Corporation.** In 2011, Olympus Corporation became entangled in Japan's biggest ever accounting scandal when its whistleblower CEO found that the company had been hiding massive investment losses.[24]

The following is perhaps the most notable of accounting scandals—Enron Corporation.

Enron Corporation

The Houston-based Enron Corporation was formed in 1985 by a merger of Houston Natural Gas Company—a $3.7 billion dollar company that had been in business since 1930—and InterNorth, a $7.5 billion company.[25] Enron went on to operate one of the largest natural gas networks on the continent and became the biggest marketer of natural gas and electricity in the country.

In 2001, however, things went south. The Securities and Exchange Commission (SEC) began investigating Enron's ousted CFO Andrew Fastow and discovered that Fastow had built a network of investment partnerships that were designed to hide the company's massive debt.[26] By the end of November, the company's stock, once worth $90, was at $1.[27]

Enron filed for bankruptcy in late 2001. It was the biggest such case in the United States up to that point. Twenty-two Enron executives were convicted or pled guilty to criminal charges as a result of the scandal.[28] Some, such as CEO Jeffrey Skilling and CFO Andrew Fastow, were given lengthy prison terms—more than 24 years for

Skilling.[29] Skilling had been charged with wire fraud, securities fraud, conspiracy, insider trading, and making false statements on financial reports. The 20,000 Enron employees lost most of their pension plans, which were tied to Enron's stock price.[30]

Whistleblowers

A *whistleblower* is an employee or other organizational insider who exposes misconduct within the organization. The term comes from sports, where a referee will blow a whistle to make a ruling of foul play.

A whistleblower may report the wrongdoing to fellow employees or superiors (internal whistleblowers), or to the media, law enforcement, or government agencies such as the Securities and Exchange Commission (SEC) or the Internal Revenue Service (IRS) (external whistleblowers).

Employees face substantial pressure to ignore wrongdoing within their companies, fearing termination, demotion, or alienation if they report misconduct. Termination may not be the worst of the repercussions, either, as the reputation of being a whistleblower may inhibit employment opportunities elsewhere.

Recognizing these fears and the need to have misconduct exposed and corrected, courts and legislatures have attempted to reduce the negative consequences of whistleblowing, and in many cases actually reward the informant. Depending upon the type of employer (e.g., public sector or private) and the state in which the employee works, the protections vary.

In what is believed to be the largest whistleblower payout of all time, an individual received $104 million in 2012 for assisting the U.S. government in a tax evasion investigation.[31] Bradley Birkenfeld, a banker at the Swiss bank UBS, helped uncover a scheme in which tens of thousands of U.S. taxpayers held undeclared amounts with the bank. Birkenfeld himself was implicated in the plot and received his payment—26 percent of $400 million in tax paid by UBS to the IRS as a result of a settlement—while serving a 40-month confinement sentence.[32]

A whistleblower protection action will generally only lie if the whistleblower faces some retaliation, usually in the form of termination or an unfavorable change in employment terms. In April 2013, a federal jury in Alaska, for instance, awarded a whistleblower $3.5 million after finding that his former employer fired him for reporting that the company was inflating its bills to the U.S. Army.[33]

Unethical conduct in the private and public sectors is a reality, and sophisticated companies have a whistleblower policy in place that engenders comfort in reporting concerns. An employee who feels secure enough to go to a superior about possible misconduct theoretically would not feel the need to go to outside authorities and create a more complicated and costly issue. An internal resolution, if possible, could not only save the company significant time and money, but would also serve to protect its reputation.

A whistleblower policy may contain several aspects. The policy could:

- Designate an ombudsman or other specific individuals or groups to receive complaints.
- Establish a fair, complete, and impartial investigative process.
- Guarantee anonymity, confidentiality, and protection from adverse employment consequences, which are most important.

Companies that have such a policy should communicate the policy to employees. They should also demonstrate that top-level managers are committed to upholding the policy.

Corporate misconduct is not going away. Increasing statutory penalties and regulatory oversight make it necessary for companies, and those in the public sector, to be as knowledgeable and prepared as possible regarding whistleblowers.

Chapter 5

PUBLIC COMPANY REPORTING

Board-shareholder communication is not a new concept. Shareholders have always been interested in the companies they own, but before the 1990s, their power to influence change in governance was limited. Investors would elect board directors to represent them, and the directors would hire management to run the company. Investors would speak with the managers instead of the directors, who would only communicate in times of crisis.

Landmark events such as the founding of the Council of Institutional Investors in 1985, the "Avon Letter" in 1988, and the repeal of the Securities and Exchange Commission's position that executive pay was "ordinary business" paved the way for greater board transparency. But it was the fraud or bankruptcies of major companies such as Enron Corporation, WorldCom, and Tyco International that prompted more direct action. In 2002, the Sarbanes-Oxley Act restructured the way public companies were required to list their stock, and turned the establishment of an independent board into a business requirement.

Thanks to the increase in Internet usage in the 1990s, the founding of the SEC's Regulation Fair Disclosure (Reg. FD) in

2000, and the passage of the Dodd-Frank Wall Street Reform and Consumer Protection Act in 2010, among other actions, boards and shareholders are more active than ever. Recent studies show that up to 76.4 percent of total U.S. equities are owned by institutional investors.[1] Shareholders believe more strongly that directors are their elected representatives, and want to go beyond traditional forms of communication.

Stephen M. Davis, a senior fellow at Harvard Law School's Program on Corporate Governance, anticipates four major changes in board-shareholder communication in the wake of the Dodd-Frank Act:

- ► The obsolescence of the noncompliance culture.
- ► A mandatory nonbinding "say on pay" vote prompting more open communication.
- ► Change in board composition through majority rule votes and shareholder action.
- ► The inclusion of social media.[2]

Change has not come easy. According to the National Investor Relations Institute (NIRI) in its 2013 Board-Shareholder Engagement Surveys, 60 percent of respondents state their companies do not permit board members to engage directly with the shareholders, and within those that do, only 65 percent allow any member to speak directly to shareholders and 35 percent state only certain directors can.

The most likely venues for direct interactions between board members and shareholders are at annual meetings (49%), through the proxy voting arms of institutional shareholders (11%), during nondeal roadshows/one-on-one meetings (9%), and at analyst days (8%). Boards that did meet directly with shareholders did so on an average of five times between 2011 and 2013, with at least one of those meetings prompted by the investor.[3]

Shareholders are demanding more and more direct contact; these assertions are supported by the passage of Reg. FD and the Dodd-Frank Act. It is important for boards to placate these concerns. As owners, shareholders have a right to dictate how their money is being spent, and, while votes are nonbinding, not siding with a popular shareholder sentiment can cost a director his or her seat on the board. It is also important to proceed with caution, or risk violating the Reg. FD's requirement that all investors receive market-moving information at the same time.

The solution is not more detailed disclosure, but *more effective* disclosure.[4] To foster this open stream of communication, public companies should establish an effective procedure for shareholders to communicate with the board or one of its committees, such as a nominating and corporate governance committee.[5] These directors and managers should make an effort to stay on top of hot issues such as proxy access, director nominations, majority voting, CEO succession, compensation, corporate strategy, and board composition.

The NACD Blue Ribbon Commission recommends all directors prepare to become more active in communications, including the annual meetings, and in individual meeting requests regarding issues that could have material impact on the company.[6] Press releases and summaries of conference calls should be available on the company website and through its social media channels.[7]

The mind-set of the investor needs to change, as well. A 2012 report from Activist Insight showed that activists in most cases got what they wanted, but the short-term goals of activist investors may not be the best decision for a long-term investment. A more typical request comes from major investors who are not branded as "activists" but take the initiative to request an opportunity to meet with directors, largely over board governance issues.

It is important for the board to keep its investors informed, as showcased by the ongoing work between the California Public Employees' Retirement System (CalPERS) and UnitedHealth Group. As part of a litigation settlement, UnitedHealth and CalPERS reached an agreement: UnitedHealth would allow shareholders access to the board member selection process, including identifying, vetting, and nominating candidates. The process relied on a set of clear steps supported by the consensus and communication that followed a regular, frequent schedule, and was to be led by active, and engaged parties. This open and frequent information produced a framework of trust and allowed the cooperation to identify and correct misunderstandings quickly. It was important for shareholders to have a comprehensive understanding of the company's near- and long-term business goals, so that everyone involved in the voting was included in the achievement strategy.

The candidates themselves were plotted along a skills matrix outlining strengths and weaknesses within the board's current membership, while reflecting the board's requirements for effective oversight. This matrix was easy for shareholders to understand, and opened discussion among the investors. It was important for the nominating committee to carefully consider these shareholder perspectives when conducting a thorough search.

Through this process, UnitedHealth has added five new directors to their board, with each appointment widely approved by annual shareholder votes. The company has seen growth in performance despite trying economic times, and expects growth to continue well into the future.[8] If not a model for better board-shareholder communication, the UnitedHealth plan may provide a starting point for other companies.

AMERICAN SECURITIES REGULATION AND THE SEC

The federal government, if you look at it benignly, serves to protect us and to help us prosper. The U.S. Securities and Exchange Commission (SEC) takes that job seriously as it enforces securities laws and regulates the securities industry. The mission of the SEC and American securities[9] regulation in general "is to protect investors, maintain fair, orderly, and efficient markets, and facilitate capital formation."[10]

The SEC explains its basic approach to securities regulation as follows: "All investors, whether large institutions or private individuals, should have access to certain basic facts about an investment prior to buying it, and as long as they hold it."[11] The regulations described below will demonstrate this approach. Increasingly, the government has sought to remedy securities problems by requiring companies to make more disclosures to investors.

The SEC's Responsibilities

The SEC was initially put in place to enforce the new securities laws of 1933 and 1934, to promote stability in the markets and, most importantly, to protect investors.[12] Companies offering securities to the public were now required to be honest about their businesses and the securities they were offering, and brokers and dealers had to deal fairly and honestly with investors, putting their interests first. It was the SEC's responsibility to enforce these rules.

Since then, securities laws, as described below, have been expanded. With more securities laws have come more regulatory duties for the SEC. In furtherance of its mission, to protect investors, the SEC makes corporate reports available to the public, offers publications on investment-related advice for public education, and takes tips and complaints from citizens.

Organization of the SEC

The SEC chairman is one of five presidentially appointed SEC commissioners who serve staggered, five-year terms. There can only be three commissioners from the same political party. Although appointed by the president, the president cannot remove commissioners—a rule enacted to ensure agency's independence.

The SEC is staffed by 3,500 employees who work in Washington, DC, and in 11 regional offices. It has five divisions: Corporation Finance, Investment Management, Trading and Markets, Enforcement, and Economic and Risk Analysis.

Securities Regulation Review

Securities regulation has likely been around as long as securities themselves. In the thirteenth century, for instance, King Edward I of England mandated that brokers in London be subject to licensing requirements. Following are some of the major securities laws enacted in the United States, as outlined in Figure 5.1.

FIGURE 5.1 The Convergence of Law and Governance

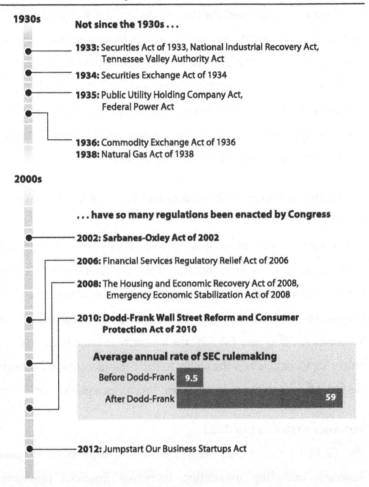

1930s

Not since the 1930s . . .

1933: Securities Act of 1933, National Industrial Recovery Act,
Tennessee Valley Authority Act

1934: Securities Exchange Act of 1934

1935: Public Utility Holding Company Act,
Federal Power Act

1936: Commodity Exchange Act of 1936
1938: Natural Gas Act of 1938

2000s

. . . have so many regulations been enacted by Congress

2002: Sarbanes-Oxley Act of 2002

2006: Financial Services Regulatory Relief Act of 2006

2008: The Housing and Economic Recovery Act of 2008,
Emergency Economic Stabilization Act of 2008

**2010: Dodd-Frank Wall Street Reform and Consumer
Protection Act of 2010**

Average annual rate of SEC rulemaking

Before Dodd-Frank 9.5

After Dodd-Frank 59

2012: Jumpstart Our Business Startups Act

Financial reform has changed the regulatory landscape in the governance industry,
heightening government expectations for oversight.
Source: For SEC Rulemaking Rate is the Committee on Capital Markets Regulation
Chart by Tom Bakewell based on an NACD chart by Peggy Heeg at *Energy Industry*.

The 1930s and 1940s was a time of great activity for securities legislation. Examples include: the development of Blue Sky Laws in the
early 1900s, the Securities Act of 1933, the Securities Exchange Act
of 1934, Investment Company Act of 1940, and Investment Advisers
Act of 1940. They were all effectively designed to protect investors.

Securities Investor Protection Act of 1970

The Securities Investor Protection Act of 1970 was enacted to reduce investor insecurity and encourage participation in the market. To achieve this goal, the act created a nonprofit entity called the Securities Investor Protection Corporation (SIPC), which protects investors from financial harm if a brokerage firm fails. One of the ways this is accomplished is by providing up to $500,000 in insurance coverage for a customer's net equity balance.

Securities Enforcement Remedies and Penny Stock Reform Act of 1990

The Securities Enforcement Remedies and Penny Stock Reform Act of 1990 is known as "the Remedies Act." This act authorized federal courts and, in administrative proceedings against regulated entities, the SEC, to hand down substantial fines for violations of federal securities laws. The Remedies Act also gave the SEC the authority to issue cease and desist orders for violations and the ability to bar persons convicted of securities fraud from serving as an officer or director of a publicly held firm.

Sarbanes-Oxley Act of 2002

The Sarbanes-Oxley Act reformed several aspects of corporate America, including mandating increased financial disclosures, enhancing corporate responsibility, and reducing corporate and accounting fraud. There will be more on this critical piece of legislation later in this chapter.

Dodd-Frank Wall Street Reform and Consumer Protection Act of 2010

President Barack Obama signed the Dodd-Frank Act into law in response to the financial crisis of the late 2000s. The goal of the act was to improve regulatory areas such as consumer protection, trading restrictions, credit ratings, regulation of financial products, corporate governance, and transparency.

Among other advancements, Dodd-Frank created the Consumer Financial Protection Bureau (CFPB). The CFPB regulates credit, debit and prepaid cards, payday and consumer loans, as well as credit reporting, debt collection, and financial advisory services. Perhaps most important, the CFPB protects consumers in home real estate transactions by mandating that borrowers fully understand what they are getting into.

SARBANES-OXLEY ACT (SOX) AND GREED IN AMERICA

Perhaps more than any other act in recent times, the Sarbanes-Oxley Act of 2002 changed the way the government policed corporate America. Accordingly, it deserves more scrutiny. The act increased mandated financial disclosures, enhanced corporate responsibility, and attempted to reduce corporate and accounting fraud.

These reforms are viewed as a legislative reaction to major corporate scandals such as those affecting Enron Corporation and Tyco International. Sarbanes-Oxley was born out of corporate greed and accounting schemes for which—up to that point—the repercussions were too weak to serve as deterrents.

Corporate scandals came in waves in the early 2000s. The Enron and Arthur Andersen LLP debacle came to a head in late 2001, along with fallouts at somewhat smaller companies like ImClone Systems Inc. and Global Crossing Ltd. Congress took little action other than holding hearings and proposing bills that went nowhere, perhaps because of an impasse between a Democratic Senate and a Republican House of Representatives.

In 2002, Tyco International, WorldCom, and Adelphia Communications Corporation all had corporate scandals come to light. The scandals, as with that of Enron, generally involved overpaid executives and accounting schemes that hid underperforming companies.

Examples of executive compensation at the disgraced companies include:

- ▶ **Enron Corporation.** In 2000, the year before declaring bankruptcy, Enron paid its top five executives $282.7 million—"completely out of whack" with its financial results, according to *Forbes* magazine.[13]

- ▶ **Tyco International.** Tyco CEO Dennis Kozlowski, along with Tyco's CFO, allegedly received $100 million in compensation that was not approved by the Tyco Board.[14] Kozlowski's alleged misuses of company funds—famously expensing a $6,000 shower curtain—were a central theme of his eventual trial.[15]

- ▶ **Adelphia Communications Corporation.** Adelphia CEO and Chairman John J. Rigas withdrew so much money from the company for personal expenses that his son, the company's CFO, had to "limit" the CEO's withdrawals to $1 million per month—a limit that was always hit.[16]

In the several corporate scandals of the early 2000s, the extraordinary compensation and personal spending were almost always accompanied by accounting gimmicks, or outright fraud, that covered up poor financial results.

With the stock market suffering, Congress acted rapidly to implement ideas that earlier had been shot down. To restore public confidence in the reliability of financial accounting and reporting, and in the financial markets in general, the Senate and the House of Representatives passed Sarbanes-Oxley by votes of 99-0 and 423-3, respectively.[17]

President George W. Bush signed the measure into law on July 30, 2002, describing it as:

> . . . the most far-reaching reforms of American business practices since the time of Franklin Delano Roosevelt. This new law sends very clear messages that all concerned must heed. This law says to every dishonest corporate leader: "You will be exposed and punished. The era of low standards and false profits is over. No boardroom in America is above or beyond the law."[18]

Under Sarbanes-Oxley, executives must individually certify the accuracy and completeness of their company's financial reports. Penalties for fraud, including criminal sanctions, are severe. Executives and directors are also barred from taking personal loans from their companies.

Sarbanes-Oxley also focuses on responsibility in accounting and auditing. The act established the Public Company Accounting Oversight Board to provide independent oversight of public accounting firms conducting audits. The act also established standards for external auditor independence to limit conflicts of interest.

Sarbanes-Oxley protects individuals who come forward with violations of the act or other laws. Specifically:

- ▶ Public companies must establish whistleblower complaint procedures and protect the confidentiality of whistleblower employees.

- ▶ The law *requires* attorneys to blow the whistle on their clients in some circumstances.
- ▶ Retaliation against whistleblowers, at companies that are publicly traded or not, is criminalized.
- ▶ The SEC has enforcement power over any aspect of the law, including the whistleblower provisions, and has the power to levy criminal sanctions.

The law also closed loopholes that allowed corporate wrongdoers to hide their tracks by shredding problematic documents. Partly in response to Arthur Andersen's destruction of Enron-related documents,[19] which drew a conviction under prior, looser obstruction of justice laws, Sarbanes-Oxley criminalizes any knowing destruction, concealment, or alteration of documents with the intent to impede an existing or contemplated investigation. Other miscellaneous provisions intended to protect shareholders include: accelerating the timeline that company insiders have for reporting stock trades and mandating that companies either disclose their ethical code or disclose their reasons for not having one.

FINANCIAL ACCOUNTING STANDARDS BOARD (FASB)

Accounting standards are vital to a market that relies on the transparency, credibility, and accuracy of corporate financial information. The Financial Accounting Standards Board (FASB) is the primary body in the United States that sets accounting standards. The FASB is made up of seven independent members, all accounting professionals. Another board, the Federal Accounting Standards Advisory Board (FASAB), publishes the *FASAB Handbook*, which is updated often, and is available on its website, www.fasab.gov.[20]

Accounting standards boost confidence in the fairness of markets, allow for proper evaluation by investors, and assist in corporate governance. They allow boards to properly evaluate management and take corrective action, when necessary.

The FASB's standards are unique to the United States, at least nominally. The International Accounting Standards Board's (IASB) international financial reporting standards have been adopted in over 100 countries, including almost all of Europe.[21] The IASB consists of 14 independent members, 12 full-time members, and 2 part-time members.[22]

Globalization has led world leaders to the belief that multinational companies should play by the same accounting rules. The FASB and the IASB have been working together since 2002 to achieve accounting consistency.[23]

Of primary importance are the FASB's generally accepted accounting principles (GAAP). GAAP are a set of rules that companies use to compile their financial statements, allowing for investors to have some confidence that the numbers can fairly and accurately be compared to those of other companies. GAAP rules have been issued over time by the FASB through its periodic "Statements of the Financial Accounting Standards."

Accounting standards did not originate with the FASB, which was created in 1973. The Securities Act of 1933 and the broader Securities Exchange Act of 1934 both allowed the Securities and Exchange Commission to prescribe accounting methods and the form and content of financial statements to be filed under the acts. Before the FASB was around, the Committee on Accounting Procedure (1936–1959) and the Accounting Principles Board (1959–1973) of the American Institute of Certified Public Accountants (AICPAs) assisted the SEC in creating accounting standards.[24]

The FASB is a private, nonprofit organization, although it cannot exactly be described as wholly independent from the government. The technical, detailed nature of accounting practices has led the SEC to outsource the standardization of accounting practices and designate the FASB as the organization responsible for setting accounting standards for public companies in the United States. Along with AICPA, the SEC officially recognizes the FASB's standards as authoritative.

The FASB is not all powerful. It operates directly under the SEC's oversight, and the SEC and Congress have the ability to dissuade or prevent accountants and companies from using the standards—meaning they would no longer be "standards." This oversight essentially gives the SEC and Congress veto power over proposed or current FASB standards, and significant influence over the enacted standards.

PUBLIC COMPANY ACCOUNTING OVERSIGHT BOARD (PCAOB)

Headquartered in Washington, D.C., but with regional offices around the country, the Public Company Accounting Oversight Board (PCAOB) is a private-sector, nonprofit corporation that provides oversight of external auditors for public companies. The board was established under Sarbanes-Oxley. Previously external auditors were self-regulated. Accounting firms that prepare audit reports for any public company *or* that play a "substantial role" in preparing a public company audit are required to register with the PCAOB.

The PCAOB is made up of five full-time members, including a chairperson, that are all on five-year staggered terms. The SEC appoints the members with input from the chairman of the Board of Governors of the Federal Reserve System and the secretary of the treasury. The board regularly holds open meetings, announced at least five days in advance, at its headquarters in Washington, D.C., to consider and vote on rulemaking and other activities.[25]

One controversial aspect of the board's makeup is that it can only include two certified public accountants (CPAs), and the PCAOB chair must not have practiced as a CPA for at least the last five years. This independence measure has caused members of the accounting industry to question how they can be assured that the non-CPAs on the board have a full understanding of the practical issues facing the accounting industry.[26]

The SEC has general oversight over the PCAOB, including veto power over the board's rules, standards, and budget, and the ability to appoint or remove members. The PCAOB also must submit an annual report (including its audited financial statements) to the SEC.[27]

The PCAOB's primary activities include:

- Registering public accounting firms
- Establishing auditing, independence, and ethical standards for auditors of public companies
- Ensuring accounting firms comply with Sarbanes-Oxley
- Investigating and disciplining noncomplying accounting firms

The board's powers include the ability to regulate the nonaudit services provided to a company that is also being audited. This power stems from the Enron and WorldCom collapses, in which the auditors' independence was questioned when they received large fees for nonaudit services.

The SEC sets the PCAOB's budget. The primary source of funding for the PCAOB is an "accounting support fee" due from companies, dealers, and brokers that are subject to the PCAOB's oversight. Larger companies, which generally involve more complex audits, pay higher fees.

The PCAOB confidentially investigates accounting firms that are not in compliance with Sarbanes-Oxley, PCAOB rules, SEC rules, and other professional standards. Disciplinary proceedings are also confidential, but sanctions, once final, may become public. Appeals of disciplinary proceedings go to the SEC. Sanctions may include fines, suspension of a firm's registration, or requiring additional training or modification within a firm.

PROXY ADVISORY SERVICES

Investors sometimes have a difficult time keeping up with all their investments. And yet, they are often called upon to cast a vote. As a result, proxy advisory services have grown substantially.

A *proxy* is generally defined as a person authorized to act on behalf of another, especially in a voting capacity. In a typical corporate context, shareholders who do not attend a company's annual meeting may choose to vote their shares "by proxy." In doing so, they appoint a third party to cast votes on their behalf.

Given that shareholders are often unable to attend the company's annual meetings in person, company executives and management encourage shareholders to vote by proxy so that ownership interests are fully represented. This issue has become a greater concern because the number of opportunities for shareholders to cast votes on various corporate governance items has increased in recent years, largely through shareholder proposals and legally mandated votes.

Many shareholders, including institutional shareholders—like mutual funds, pension funds, endowments, and insurance companies—simply do not have the requisite knowledge to make an informed decision on complicated corporate governance issues. Institutional investors play a special role as fiduciaries for the actual owners of the assets being invested. This fiduciary relationship creates duties of care and loyalty that involve the exercise of their shares' voting rights.

This leads many institutional investors to believe that farming the necessary research out (and in many cases, the voting decision itself) to third parties is the most cost-efficient way to meet their duties. This position is fueled by the SEC, which has stated that the use of informed third-party recommendations developed by independent third parties is sufficient to meet voting obligations.

These third parties are known as "proxy advisory firms" or "proxy firms." For a price, these companies engage in data collection and research, and then advise institutional shareholders by way of formal written opinions, often referred to as "proxy advisory reports."

In issuing written opinions and reports, proxy advisors are generally serving as third-party advisors. Proxy advisory firms are *not* voting shares in their own right. They are providing research, advice, and opinions related to corporate elections for clients that have hired them for a fee. Each proxy advisory firm has its own proprietary factors, approaches, and methodologies that are used to analyze the proposals and give advice.

Advice generally touches upon whether or not shareholders ought to support or oppose specific matters and proposals submitted for a vote, usually at the companies' annual shareholders meeting or at a special meeting. In some instances, proxy advisors will actually cast the proxy votes on their clients' behalf.

Proxy advisory firms recommend how to vote on the specific matters and proposals coming to a vote based upon their research, review, and evaluation of a company's public disclosures and practices regarding the proposal in question. The proxy advisor often casts its recommendation in relation or comparison to the recommendation of the company's management or its board of directors.

Recommendations by proxy advisors to vote for or against any particular matter—technically a vote can be for, against, or to withhold a vote—are generally followed by the companies who request such advice. A Stanford University study found that a proxy advisor's recommendation to oppose a proposed measure results in a "20 percent increase in negative votes cast."[28] The figure may actually under-represent the effect of proxy advisors, as companies may only propose initiatives that they believe proxy advisors will recommend.

Much of the work of proxy advisory firms deals with routine corporate elections, although ideally they work to help manage critical governance risks for the benefit of the company's shareholders. Generally, the matters and proposals reviewed are select shareholder matters like votes on the company's board of directors, executive compensation pay practices, ratifying election of the company's auditors, and other good governance factors.

The advice from proxy advisory firms can capture a great deal of public attention. Here are a few examples:

▶ *Apple.* In 2014, a proxy advisory firm recommended that Apple shareholders reject Carl Icahn's shareholder proposal that Apple spend an additional $50 billion in share buybacks.[29]

▶ *Dell Inc.* In 2013, three proxy advisory firms recommended that Dell Inc.'s stockholders vote to accept the controversial $24.4 billion buyout offer of founder Michael Dell, who sought to take the company private.[30]

▶ *JPMorgan Chase & Co.* In 2012, a major proxy advisory firm recommended a proposal for voting to divest JPMorgan Chase & Co. CEO Jamie Dimon of his joint chairman role, which he had long held.[31] Also in 2012, two proxy advisory firms sought votes against the reelection of three directors serving on JPMorgan Chase's risk committee, alleging that they failed to adequately oversee the bank's risk and noting that directors with more specialized experience in risk management were needed.[32] Each of these recommendations came after enormous trading losses known now as "the London Whale."

▶ *J.Crew Group, Inc.* In 2011, a proxy advisory firm recommended that J. Crew Group, Inc. shareholders reject a sale of the company to a private group that included the company's CEO.[33]

▶ *Dynegy Inc.* In 2010, a proxy advisory firm urged investors to reject a takeover of Houston, Texas–based public utility and energy company Dynegy Inc. by way of a merger agreement with an affiliate of The Blackstone Group LP.[34]

The advice is not always taken. Jamie Dimon retained his joint CEO and chairman roles, although an independent lead director was added at JPMorgan Chase, and the three incumbent directors were reelected in close votes. J. Crew was sold to a private group including the CEO. The Dynegy merger agreement was not approved, possibly due to a bankruptcy filing hanging in the balance. Dell stockholders voted, and the company became private in 2013.

There are some common criticisms of proxy advisory firms:

- ► Their use of "one-size-fits-all" guidelines. Proxy advisory firms cannot possibly get to know the unique ins and outs of specific companies, and thus often fall back on generic positions.
- ► They are not shareholders and therefore do not directly bear the cost of bad decisions.
- ► They generally remain unregulated and unsupervised, and are not transparent with regard to procedures, their own compensation, standards, and conflicts of interest.
- ► They are criticized as suffering from conflicts of interest. Some of their biggest clients are large pension plans run by unions and politically motivated individuals with strong social, labor, and environmental agendas. Other clients are public corporations—known as "issuers"—who the advisory firms advise on governance policy (e.g., how to get proxy questions approved).

Proxy Advisory Services and Reports

Proxy advisory groups prepare reports that explain their opinions and recommendations for upcoming votes. The reports are meant to provide shareholders with the information necessary to make informed votes on issues vital to the company's performance. Proxy reports are thought to offer shareholders and prospective investors tremendous insight into a company's governance as well as a glance at the way that a company's management operates.

The typical proxy advisory report provides a review of the company's key profile information, current matters being reviewed, and other items. The following is a rundown of some specific issues included in the reports:

▸ An industry profile
▸ Meeting dates
▸ The company's recent financial performance data
▸ Recent voting records and election results
▸ Identification of major shareholders
▸ Board composition, independence review, board member qualifications, and other board data
▸ Executive compensation and pay practices
▸ Governance matters in general
▸ A list and review of meeting agenda items and proposals at hand, along with the recommendations and opinions of the proxy advisory firm issuing the report and opinion, which are of most relevance to the proxy advisory process

Proxy advisory firms include:

▸ Glass, Lewis & Co., LLC
▸ Institutional Shareholder Services (ISS)
▸ Egan-Jones Proxy Services
▸ PROXY Governance, Inc.
▸ The Marco Consulting Group (MCG)
▸ C&W Investment Group, Inc.

Glass, Lewis & Co., LLC, and Institutional Shareholders Services have long been the largest providers of proxy advisory services. Third-party risk assessments are described in Figure 5.2.

FIGURE 5.2 Third-Party Risk Assessments

BOARD STRUCTURE

Evaluation of the way the board is structured, including, but not limited to:

- What is the board composition?
- How are the committees composed?
- What are the board practices?
- What are the board policies?

COMPENSATION

Evaluation of board compensation, including, but not limited to:

- Is there pay for performance?
- Nonperformance-based pay
- Use of equity
- Equity risk mitigation
- What is the nonexecutive pay?
- Communications and disclosure
- Are there controversies?

SHAREHOLDER RIGHTS

Evaluation of shareholder rights, including, but not limited to:

- One share, one vote
- What are their takeover defenses?
- Are there voting issues?
- What are the voting formalities?

AUDIT

Evaluation of the way the board is audited, including, but not limited to:

- Is there an external auditor?
- Have there been audit and accounting controversies?
- A look at other audit issues

Companies like consulting firms and proxy advisory firms look at different areas of a company board to assess governance risk.

Source: Sample comments based on typical third-party proxy advisory reports prepared by Tom Bakewell.

Proxy Solicitation Firms

Historically, "proxy solicitation firms" have been known to have one central purpose: to contact a client's shareholders and obtain votes on a certain measure. This remains an important aspect of their work, but proxy solicitation firms have expanded their activities.

Communication between management and shareholders is vital, but often difficult. Proxy solicitation firms purport to ease this process by *directly* seeking out shareholders and communicating with them. Ideally, correspondence with shareholders will improve shareholder participation and deter activist shareholders.

Proxy solicitation firms can help their clients analyze shareholder makeup and voting patterns, and through periodic reports, they can give clients an idea of what to expect from shareholders in anticipation of a meeting. Management then may be able to assess, before a meeting, whether a new strategy is necessary.

Proxy solicitation firms may be particularly useful if the corporation is at risk for a stealth takeover, a proxy fight, or if a hostile bid is underway for a client. Correspondence with shareholders may reveal these situations and allow the client to snuff them out.

CASE STUDY: GENERAL MOTORS GETS A NEW CEO

G. Richard "Rick" Wagoner had been chief executive officer (CEO) of General Motors (GM) since 2000 and chairman since 2003. He was asked to resign in March 2009 by the Obama administration as part of an agreement that would provide the automaker with a federal bailout.[35]

GM veteran Frederick "Fritz" Henderson was immediately elevated from chief operating officer (COO) to CEO to replace Wagoner. President Obama's auto czar Steven Rattner then asked Edward E. Whitacre, Jr., the retired AT&T CEO and chairman, to be the new GM chairman.

Whitacre initially declined the offer, but later joined GM as chairman in July 2009 when the new company was launched with renewed federal financing. The arrangement gave the U.S. Treasury a 60 percent stake in GM and the Canadian government an 11.7 percent stake. Five new directors joined GM when Whitacre stepped in as chairman, building a reconstituted board of 13 directors.

CEO Henderson resigned in early December 2009 with Whitacre taking on that role as well on an interim basis. Whitacre was then quickly appointed permanent CEO. It has been widely reported that Whitacre orchestrated Henderson's ouster.[36]

Whitacre said he liked Henderson personally and admired his commitment to the company. But he described Henderson as a product of a broken culture incapable of changing fast. "Everybody liked Fritz, respected his deep knowledge, and greatly appreciated his many years of service," Whitacre said. "But the decision was unanimous: Fritz had to go."[37]

Whitacre served as CEO for just 9 months. Daniel Akerson took on the role of CEO in September 2010, and chairman in January 2011. He held these jobs until December 2013. In January 2014, GM insider Mary T. Barra was named CEO of the company, making her the first woman to head up a major automaker.

Questions

1. Do you see any problems with conflicts of interest in this string of successions?
2. Were these extraordinary events or business as usual for corporate America?
3. Can you suggest better options or actions for these CEO successions?

Chapter 6

ACHIEVING EXCELLENCE IN GOVERNANCE

Inevitably the concept of best practices surfaces when directors and managers take a serious look at important questions related to governance like: "How can we have the best governance possible?" or "What makes a great board great?" or "How can we fix our recent governance failure?"

The term "best practice" is a buzzword that has developed over the years to suggest there is some superior way of doing things. A best practice can:

▶ Develop from years of application in a particular industry.
▶ Come from thought leaders propounding new ideas.
▶ Come from regulatory bodies implementing new laws or standards.
▶ Develop from any number of other sources.

Numerous organizations use the concept of best practices for a wide range of purposes. Hospitals have best practices for infection control. Human resources departments have best practices for hiring. Police departments have best practices for gun safety.

Best Practices in Governance

When writing of *best practices* in the field of governance, I am referring to a focus on the leading principles and practices that can help boards, directors, and management enhance their ability to govern ever more effectively. This means asking if there are best practices that can help boards be more effective in key areas related to corporate governance like:

▶ Developing great strategy

▶ Recruiting directors

▶ Having a productive boardroom culture

▶ Having a transparent organizational culture

▶ Overseeing risk management

▶ Determining executive compensation

▶ Planning for succession

Are best practices mandatory or required by law for boards of directors? Generally speaking, best practices for boards are not mandated or required, even when there is every indication that a best practice might be a terrific idea and add great value to an organization.

To be sure, there are always some legal statutes, regulatory requirements, or related mandates that are both required and likewise considered principles of good governance or best practices.

For example, with publicly listed companies, the Dodd-Frank Wall Street Reform and Consumer Protection Act and the Sarbanes-Oxley Act (SOX) established independence standards for particular purposes (see Chapter 5). Dodd-Frank requires that a publicly listed company's compensation committee director members be independent.

With nonprofit organizations the Internal Revenue Service (IRS) in recent years has taken actions, with substantial changes to Form 990 (IRS Return of Organization Exempt from Income Tax), signaling to nonprofit organizations today that good governance is of far greater importance to them and the IRS. The IRS is saying by their actions that *good governance* means an engaged and informed board that is fully independent, acting transparently, with very clear policies and practices. The IRS's far tougher audits and enforcement standards are resulting in real fines and lost tax exemptions.

Public company boards today are intensely focused in both practice and reporting on assuring that their key board committees like compensation, audit, and nominating and governance have the required number of independent directors. Nonprofits are experiencing the dramatic new standards required by updated Form 990. I have personally advised a number of fine nonprofits that were shocked to be faced with the complexity of the new forms, the need for professional accounting or legal services to complete the forms, and the new reality of very large fines for filing inadequacies that in the past would have been resolved with a few phone calls, letters, and no fines.

Beyond these examples of statutes, regulatory requirements, and related matters, vigilant boards and directors must always be on the watch for the occasional circumstance where a law suddenly kicks a standard, principle, or best practice into the category of required, mandated, or simply requiring far more attention than in the past.

In recent years, there is little doubt that the board of directors for almost every college and university in the United States with sports programs has a new appreciation for the importance of the long-standing, often overlooked, 1972 Title IX federal law, which is best known for requiring gender equity and prohibiting sexual discrimination, including violent sexual harassment. Likewise, the Jeanne Clery Disclosure of Campus Security Policy and Campus Crime Statistics Act (better known as "the Clery Act") has in recent years dramatically raised the level of awareness for college and university boards regarding their fiduciary duties to clearly address campus culture, including sexual misconduct, given the truly unfortunate events involving the Jerry Sandusky sex abuse scandal that broke into the public eye in 2011.

The decade of 2001 to 2010 saw a dramatic increase in the amount of scrutiny placed on the oversight processes for boards, especially for public companies, which often are leading indicators of new or best practices that can be picked up and then transferred to private and nonprofit companies. These public companies had a whole new round of institutional investors, shareholder activists, and proxy advisors looking over their shoulders and suggesting new ways and best practices to run their businesses.

Given the worldwide financial crises, including the mortgage bubble collapse, a vast new array of regulators and regulations were instituted including: the Sarbanes-Oxley Act of 2002, the Financial

Services Regulatory Relief Act of 2006, the Dodd-Frank Wall Street Reform and Consumer Protection Act of 2010 (Dodd-Frank Act), and the EPA Regulatory Relief Act of 2011. Some companies actively sought out or applied new best practices. Many did not.

Board practices are developed over time, and are in many ways a function of the history of the company and the people in the executive offices and boardroom. How do they operate as a group? What practices have they developed and embraced over the years? Are their culture and style highly entrepreneurial or much more detailed and by the company manual? What do they determine is best practice for their organization? And remember, the board, in particular, oversees and does not manage.

My own experience working with boards and best practices has surfaced a number of old adages:

▸ Every organization is unique and yet there are always common themes.
▸ If you have seen one board you have seen one board, as each board is unique.
▸ Best practices are something to aspire to. If the shoe fits and it adds value, then wear it.
▸ There is no single best practice. There are many best practices. What works best for us now?

Best Practice Examples

Let's look at a few examples of companies picking the best practice that works for them. As a baseline of a well-known company's corporate governance guidelines, I will draw from the General

Motors (GM) Company Board of Directors Corporate Governance
Guidelines:

General Motors Company Board of Directors Corporate Governance Guidelines (Index)

Introduction
1. Board Mission and Responsibilities

Selection and Composition of the Board
2. Board Designation Rights under Stockholders' Agreement
3. Board Membership Criteria
4. Board Membership Selection
5. Extending the Invitation to a Potential Director to Join the Board
6. Majority Voting in Board Elections
7. Director Orientation and Continuing Education

Board Functioning
8. Selection of the Chairman of the Board and Role of Lead Director
9. Size of the Board
10. Mix of Management and Independent Directors
11. Board Definition of What Constitutes Independence for Directors
12. Former Chief Executive Officer Board Membership
13. Directors Who Change Their Present Job Responsibilities
14. Limits on Outside Board Memberships
15. Meeting Attendance

16. Retirement Age and Term Limits

17. Board Compensation

18. Loans to Directors and Executive Officers

19. Stock Ownership by Nonemployee Directors

20. Executive Sessions of Nonmanagement Directors

21. Access to Outside Advisors

22. Assessing the Board's Performance

23. Ethics and Conflicts of Interest

24. Confidentiality

25. Board Interaction with Stockholders and Other Interested Parties

Board Relationship to Senior Management

26. Regular Attendance of Nondirectors at Board Meetings

27. Board Access to Senior Management

Meeting Procedures

28. Selection of Agenda Items for Board Meetings

29. Board Materials Distributed in Advance

30. Board Presentations

Committee Matters

31. Board Committees

32. Committee Performance Evaluation

33. Assignment and Rotation of Committee Members

34. Frequency and Length of Committee Meetings

35. Committee Agenda

Leadership Development

36. Formal Evaluation of the Chief Executive Officer

37. Succession Planning

38. Management Development

These GM Governance Guidelines include 38 items and 15 pages of content available in full at the GM website, www.gm.com. The seven category headings GM uses are listed here as an overview: Introduction, Selection and Composition of the Board, Board Functioning, Board Relationship to Senior Management, Meeting Procedures, Committee Matters, and Leadership Development.

Best Practice of Former CEOs Not Serving on Their Company Boards after Retirement

This is a widely accepted best practice across public, private, and nonprofit companies. General Motors has a similar board-approved guideline (GM Item 12) on *Former Chief Executive Officer Board Membership* that states: "The Board believes that it is preferable that the CEO and senior executives of GM not serve on the Board following retirement from GM." While the GM Board has made this a formal guideline for GM, there is no special legal statute precluding CEOs from continuing board service in public companies. Many companies have a similar policy with a one-year transition period for the retiring CEO to mentor the new CEO, and some serving at the pleasure of the new CEO.

In my own experience, I worked with a billion-dollar privately held company that worked in a very "public arena," driving them, as public leaders, to be models of good governance adopting *every* best practice they could, including immediately removing retiring CEOs. After some unfortunate leadership turnovers from a string of health issues, the board found the ideal new CEO. This new CEO made it a condition of employment that a much loved and talented CEO who was retired for several years be permitted to rejoin the board. An exception to best practice was made for good cause to address particular company circumstances, and the long-term result was outstanding performance for the new CEO and company.

Interestingly, this excellent best practice of former CEOs retiring has received a lot of attention and has been particularly useful in the nonprofit arena addressing the tricky issue of former founder CEOs of important charities wanting to stay on their boards after retirement. This best practice has given clear guidance that it's best for most charities when the former founder CEO makes a clean break from the board at retirement.

Best Practice of Directors Who Change Their Job Responsibilities

A best practice growing rapidly in use over the past decade is for serving directors to submit their resignations to the board chairs whenever there is a major change to their primary work. There are many good reasons for this practice: It gives the board maximum flexibility in keeping the range of skills on the board that they need and want, especially if a director is retiring, changing careers, or taking on major new responsibilities that will compromise his or her availability. It gives the board freedom to properly address many other practical realities ranging from the routine—like a director moving thousands of miles or having a personal schedule that no longer works—to the complex—like a director moving to a company that some consider a competitor or a director facing a rocky transition from his or her current circumstances.

I like that it puts the needs of the board first and it permits the board to consider the individual circumstances on a case-by-case basis. Recent experience shows that boards use this best practice carefully and work to keep talented directors. When David S. Pottruck was terminated as CEO of Charles Schwab Corporation in 2004, he attended an Intel Corporation board meeting the next day and met with the chairman. His long-term service as a director with Intel continues beyond 2012.[1] Conversely, a respected director of the Harvard Corporation (they are known as Fellows) tendered his resignation to Harvard when his board service with Enron during their collapse drew attention. He bravely quoted a friend's advice on resigning: "You learn it's not about you at all. . . . There's nothing you can do. You have to accept that it's not about you at all."[2] It also leaves the board lots of room for discretion in dealing with the close calls in life anyone can face like scandals, company crisis, or personal challenges.

The General Motors guideline (GM Item 13) on *Directors Who Change Their Present Job Responsibilities* states:

> When a Director's principal occupation or business association changes substantially from the position he or she held when originally invited to join the Board, the Director will tender a letter of resignation to the Chairman or the Corporate Secretary. The Governance Committee will review whether the new occupation, or retirement, of the director is consistent with the Guidelines for Board Membership and the specific rationale for originally selecting that individual. The Governance Committee will recommend to the full Board whether to accept the director's resignation based on the factors that it considers relevant, which may include the circumstances of the change in employment and the director's experience with the Board and contributions to the Board's diversity of backgrounds and viewpoints, as well as whether the director was designated for nomination by a stockholder of the Company.

Best Practice of Limits on Outside Board Memberships

In the 1980s and 1990s there were a number of high-profile well-connected trophy directors serving on as many as 8 to 10 boards at a time. Vernon Jordan was reported to be on 11 boards by the *New York Times* in 1996, when a number of unions and pension funds began to question these practices.[3] At the time, it was routine for many CEOs to serve on multiple boards beyond their own companies. Lists began showing up like the "least valuable directors in corporate America," published by the International Brotherhood of Teamsters' pension fund. Along with these public criticisms, the demands on directors' time increased substantially in the post-Sarbanes-Oxley era, as did the demand on CEOs. Other best practices regarding conflicts of interest, director independence, and director attendance coalesced around the challenges of being on multiple boards and resulted in this new trend to limit outside board memberships.

The General Motors guideline (GM Item 14) on *Limits on Outside Board Memberships* is indicative of this best practice for many companies today:

> It is the expectation of the Board that every member have sufficient time to commit to preparation for and attendance at Board and committee meetings. Therefore, it is the sense of the Board that nonemployee directors should not serve on more than four other boards of publicly traded companies (excluding nonprofits and subsidiaries) unless the Board determines that such service will not impair the ability of such director to effectively perform his or her obligations as a director of the Company. In addition, no member of the Audit Committee may serve

on more than three other audit committees of publicly traded companies (excluding nonprofits and subsidiaries), unless the Board determines that such simultaneous service would not impair the ability of such member to effectively serve on the Company's Audit Committee. Directors should advise the Chairman of the Board or the Chair of the Governance Committee in advance of (i) accepting an invitation to serve on another board of directors, or (ii) significant commitments involving affiliation with other businesses or governmental units.

I also note that GM recommends their management directors serve on only one other board. This reflects two important trends. First, companies are finding great value in having their junior executives on the rise serve on a board outside their company to gain broader experience. Second, many companies today much prefer that their senior executives devote the majority of their time focused on their current company obligations. Limiting other board service to one other public company helps protect the executives from heavy outside time demands.

Best Practice in Splitting the Board Chair and CEO Roles or Having Them Combined in One Person

This was a hot topic that received wide attention in 2012 when world-class banker Jamie Dimon of the largest U.S. bank JPMorgan Chase & Co. was challenged by many proxy advisory firms and CalPERS (California Public Employees' Retirement System) to give up his long-term combined chairman and CEO role in the wake of an embarrassing and costly financial problem known as the "London

Whale" trading loss that exceeded $6 billion. A proposal barring Dimon from holding both roles made it to a shareholder vote at the bank's annual shareholder meeting in May 2013. Only a third of the shareholders voted to split Dimon's job.[4]

General Motors has a board-approved guideline that gives the board the discretion to decide based on the circumstances of the company. The General Motors Guideline (GM Item 8) *Selection of the Chairman of the Board and Role of Lead Director* states that:

> The Board should be free to choose a Chairman of the Board in the way that seems best for the Company at a given time, based on the circumstances of the Company and the individuals on the Board at that time. Therefore, the Board does not have any policy whether or not the role of the Chairman and CEO should be separate or combined and, if it is separate, whether the Chairman should be an employee or a nonemployee Director.

The GM guideline covers a good bit more, including the concept of a "lead independent director," a term also known as a "presiding director." The New York Stock Exchange (NYSE) requires that nonexecutive directors meet without management in regular executive sessions with an independent director presiding over these meetings.[5]

The position of lead independent director has emerged as somewhat of a compromise, perhaps better said solution, between allowing companies to maintain dual chair/CEO positions and forcing companies to separate these roles and appoint an independent chair. The position evolved from the role served by the director who presides over executive sessions of the board. In recent years, this director has assumed a more prominent role with expanded powers and has come to be known as the lead independent director. The term *presiding director* is still used, but is most often used to refer to the person who chairs the annual and executive session meetings required for the public exchanges. Often times, the lead director fulfills the function of presiding director as well.

Many corporate governance experts recommend that companies formally appoint a lead independent director, particularly those in which the CEO also serves as board chair. The expectation is that the lead independent director can serve as an important counterbalance to the chair/CEO. However, beyond presiding over executive sessions, the responsibilities of this role are still being defined and vary widely across companies.

According to Professor Jeffrey A. Sonnenfeld of Yale University, splitting the roles can make sense, but "it's not a panacea." There are several examples of disasters within companies where the roles were split, and in the aftermath, splitting the roles creates confusion as to who speaks for the company. There's zero research that splitting the roles is preventive or that it results in better shareholder value or governance.[6]

Best Practices Wrap: How Many Best Practices are There?

So, what is the number of best practices out there related to good governance? The General Motors Company Board of Directors Corporate Governance Guidelines, referenced earlier, has 38 items in its Index.

The GM Guidelines have been carefully honed and crafted over many years for this major public company, which has experienced almost every governance challenge imaginable, including the removal of several CEOs by the board, bankruptcy, and a federal bailout. I consider this list an excellent model of best practices for public companies by a company that has paid its dues and worked tirelessly for years to be a model of good governance.

The single-finest comprehensive list of best practices that I have seen over many years from the world of nonprofit governance has 33 items. This list uses the term "Principles" for Good Governance and Ethical Practice rather than "best practices" and has four major categories including: Legal Compliance and Public Disclosure, Effective Governance, Strong Financial Oversight, and Responsible Fundraising. This list was developed as a major research effort convened by a great organization named Independent Sector with the encouragement of the U.S. Senate Finance Committee. Work was conducted from 2004 to 2007. Another leading organization in nonprofit governance organization, named BoardSource, created added tools that resulted in this document titled *The Principles Workbook: Steering Your Board Toward Good Governance and Ethical Practice, A companion to The Principles for Good Governance and Ethical Practice: A Guide for Charities and Foundations.*

So we see GM with 38 best practices and Figure 6.1 from Independent Sector and BoardSource with 33 principles, with many of these best practices and principles covering very common ground. Any good list I have seen over the years of best practices for private company boards has closely followed the items covered in these 38 best practices and 33 Principles. Please note that fund raising is specific to nonprofits, although many public and private companies have best practices for giving company gifts to charities. If one thinks broadly about best practices and includes key detailed areas like investment management, record retention, and executive

FIGURE 6.1 Good Example of Nonprofit Best Practices

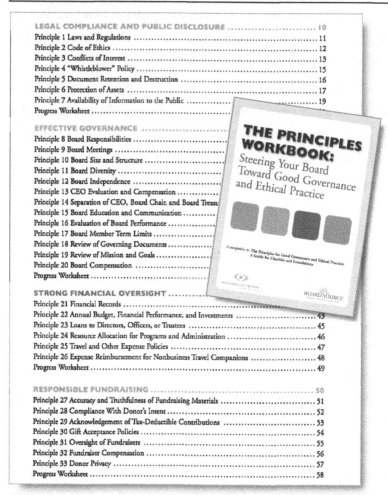

THE PRINCIPLES WORKBOOK: Steering Your Board Toward Good Governance and Ethical Practice

A companion to *The Principles for Good Governance and Ethical Practice: A Guide for Charities and Foundations*

BOARDSOURCE

This contents page from *The Principles Workbook* is a good place to start for nonprofit best practices.

compensation, it is possible to expand a list of best practices to 75 or 100 items related to good governance. I will wrap up this section on best practices by providing my own very brief descriptions of other best practices taken from the GM guidelines.

Retirement Age and Term Limits

The trend is for independent directors to offer their resignations around the age of 72, which is moving well beyond the traditional retirement age of 65. Some companies have a firm rule and others have only guidelines. Some boards have fixed term limits such as 3 terms of 3 years each and others have no term limits. In the United Kingdom, public company directors are no longer considered independent after a decade of service. It is easy to find renowned directors with great longevity—like Warren Buffett, Charlie Munger, and Carl Icahn—still active on their company boards.

Board Compensation

Employee directors seldom receive added fee compensation for board service with their company. Independent directors of public and private companies often receive fees as retainers or attendance fees, including expense reimbursement. Public company directors often receive stock awards, which vest over time as some portion of their fee. Private company directors most always receive cash fees, as private company owners are not inclined to dilute their ownership. Nonprofits rarely pay directors fees, although there are some notable exceptions of nonprofit boards that pay nicely, like some of the large health care company boards. Many nonprofits do reimburse some expenses, and most always welcome their directors to make charitable donations to the nonprofit. It is important to have clear board compensation policies that will stand up to close scrutiny.

Access to Outside Advisors

Boards and committees find value in having the right and power to hire outside advisors at company expense when needed for counsel on legal, financial, and banking issues. A recent example of using outside advisors involved the decision by Michael Dell, in 2012, to pursue a management buyout of the public company Dell Inc. Once Michael Dell told the board of directors that he wanted to take Dell private with a purchase of the public company shares, the board needed to create a special committee of independent directors to handle the potential sale process of negotiating with Michael Dell and other potential purchasers. This required extensive counsel from many outside advisors.

Ethics and Conflicts of Interest

Good ethics are important for any company. Directors and employees have an obligation to keep the board informed of any potential or real personal conflicts of interest they have related to the company. If the conflict of interest involved cannot be properly resolved, and it involves a significant conflict, the director may need to resign from the board.

Confidentiality

Information revealed to directors is considered confidential and may not be disclosed beyond the boardroom, unless the information is intended to be public or has become public in some proper way. Directors have the duty to keep confidential information private during and after their service.

Board Access to Senior Management

It is considered valuable for the board to come to know key members of the management team beyond the CEO. Some companies strive to make time for the directors to meet and mingle with the management by including senior managers in board meetings, or inviting them to meals or social events with directors. Various companies have different protocols for directors interacting with management, such as scheduling all meetings through the CEO or lead director, or copying the CEO on all correspondence.

BENCHMARKING

Benchmarking is a concept closely linked to best practices. The terms are at times used to describe the same or similar concepts. *Benchmarking* is the process of seeking to identify and establish some particular defined standard baseline to measure against. Benchmarking seeks to measure, on a comparative basis, how you or your organization measures up against the baseline you have selected to measure. As mentioned with best practices, numerous organizations use the concept of benchmarking for a wide range of purposes throughout their organizations like: universities touting their student-faculty ratios as a perceived measure of quality, hospitals advertising their short emergency room waiting times, and car companies highlighting their latest industry quality award.

In my own consulting experience, I have learned that the best benchmarking always starts with having an organization benchmarking against itself. That means measuring your own organization's results internally at different points in time to see if your company is on a good trajectory toward an improved goal, or going nowhere fast. Benchmarking internally provides the added benefit of the team learning about the complexities of benchmarking, so that when it comes time to benchmark externally, there tends to be a better understanding in finding good comparative benchmarks.

Once you have established a good internal baseline benchmark for your organization in some particular area, then you can seek outside resources and companies to benchmark against. Often there are associations, consultants, or vendors that maintain specific types of benchmarking data.

The benchmarks you select to measure good governance can be objective and very quantitative or subjective and very qualitative. The range of benchmarks used is only limited by your creativity and imagination.

Examples of objective and quantitative benchmarking for a board could include director compensation for public, private, and nonprofit organizations. Public companies have detailed, robust databases to draw from multiple sources to use in comparing directors' fees on many indexes or benchmarks like annual revenues, asset size, industry classification, and more. This is what you might expect for public companies, which are required to publish a great amount of data in their regular regulatory reporting.

Private companies have a very limited amount of data on director compensation. A handful of consulting and search firms have some good information on private company director compensation that they do share with clients.

Nonprofits seldom provide director compensation. Indeed, most people naturally assume that the nature of a nonprofit precludes director compensation. All the same there have been, for years, a handful of nonprofits in particular industries or with certain legal structures that provide director compensation, with some directors paid generously. This information has been closely guarded in past years but, with the IRS requiring substantially more disclosure in tax forms, it can also be obtained by directly accessing the tax forms.

Examples of subjective and qualitative benchmarking for a board could include the desire to comparatively measure a board on three soft topics like: having a capable board, having strong board performance, and having excellent succession planning for the CEO and board. This could be measured internally by:

- ▶ Asking the board to score itself, year over year, on adding people with key skills targeted for having a capable board.
- ▶ Measuring overall board performance on some simple targeted measures or index, like working well together or growing the organization.
- ▶ Meeting a goal of having a written CEO and board succession plan in writing and reviewed by the board twice a year.

These could also be measured on an external basis by a third party conducting interviews or surveys.

A few closing words on benchmarking are in order. When using comparative external objective data from outside sources and other organizations, always be aware that the quality and accuracy of the data can vary widely and requires careful review. I have in mind a number of experiences with both director and executive compensation external databases that were represented as the ideal benchmark for a small regional nursing home chain, when in fact the benchmark was from much larger major national health care organizations. Of course, it was a simple oversight of a consultant in preparing the data, or so they claimed. Likewise, I regularly see industry benchmarks that strive to reflect comparative data like labor as a percent of net revenues, where major components of the labor are contracted out by key players creating skewed numbers. Finally, don't resist the use of really simple measures or indexes of a subjective nature, like having a capable board. They really can provide great insights for good governance.

CEO COMMITMENT AND BOARD LEADERSHIP

A key ingredient to achieving success with good governance is having a CEO who is actively committed to both the ideals and hard work of investing the time, energy, and resources over a number of years—often decades—to develop good governance practices. Good governance is an ongoing process that can produce great results over time with the proper commitment and support from the company. Inevitably, strong, steady leadership from the CEO is a key element in determining if a company's efforts to enhance governance over time will produce strong results, or not. The CEO will set the tone for a collaborative relationship with the leadership of the board. And let's be plain and realistic. Talented directors and CEOs often have strong personalities and opinions. Sharing power in the boardroom is very often a long-term challenge even in the best of circumstances.

Another key ingredient to success with good governance is clarity for the board and organization on board leadership. There are many approaches or models that can be used for board leadership:

- ► Will there be a common board chair and CEO, as was most common for past decades with the majority of public companies?
- ► Will there be an independent board chair separate from the CEO, as is most prevalent today with public companies? This has long been the common model for the majority of nonprofit boards.

▶ Will there be other modified approaches, like a lead director or presiding director working in concert with a common board chair and CEO?

Great board leadership comes from the CEO and the board working in concert to determine a unified approach that proves effective for meeting the unique needs of their board. The best boards have a clear leader emerge over time from the regular work and events of the board. Ideally, that leadership is based on trust and candor, and not just power. Having a board chair who is skilled at facilitation and administrative follow-up is important. One of the greatest skills for any board chair is the ability to be sure that everybody in the room is heard, even when faced with limited time and critically important discussions. Figure 6.2 details the relationship of the leader of the independent directors and the CEO.

The strongest boards develop a vital social system where the directors are able to work together, in concert with management, as a robust collective body. Yes, the policies and procedures of the board are important. But how the board learns to work together, in good times and bad, is far more important than any set of rules or regulations.

Key elements in setting the stage for success with strong board leadership include a well-thought-out division of responsibilities and duties between the board chair and CEO roles. This includes written responsibilities for the board chair, that relate clearly with the CEO's job description, which are approved by the board. A specific predetermined tenure or term limit for the board chair is important to the integrity of the process.

A strong evaluation process for the CEO, board, and the board chair on a regular basis goes a long way toward building trust,

FIGURE 6.2 Relationship of the Leader of the Independent Directors and the CEO

Areas of Responsibility	CHAIR/CEO MODEL		NONEXECUTIVE CHAIR MODEL
	Chair/CEO Role	Lead Director Role	Nonexecutive Chair Role
Full Board Meetings	• Has the authority to call meetings of the board of directors. • Chairs meetings of the board of directors and the annual meeting of shareholders.	• Participates in board meetings like every other director. • Acts as intermediary—at times, the chair may refer to the lead director for guidance or to have something taken up in executive session. • Suggests calling full board meetings to the chair when appropriate.	• Has the authority to call meetings of the board of directors. • Chairs meetings of the board of directors and the annual meeting of shareholders (although in some cases the CEO chairs in the presence of the nonexecutive chair).
Executive Sessions	• Receives feedback from the executive sessions.	• Has the authority to call meetings of the independent directors. • Sets the agenda for and leads executive sessions of the independent directors. • Briefs the CEO on issues arising in the executive sessions.	• Has the authority to call meetings of the independent directors. • Sets the agenda for and leads executive sessions of the independent directors. • Briefs the CEO on issues arising in the executive sessions.
Board Agendas and Information	• Takes primary responsibility for shaping board agendas, consulting with the lead director to ensure that board agendas and information provide the board with what is needed to fulfill its primary responsibilities.	• Collaborates with the chair/CEO to set the board agenda and board information. • Seeks agenda input from other directors.	• Takes primary responsibility for shaping board agendas in collaboration with the CEO. • Consults with all directors to ensure that board agendas and information provide the board with what is needed to fulfill its primary responsibilities.
Board Communications	• Communicates with all directors on key issues and concerns outside of board meetings.	• Facilitates discussion among the independent directors on key issues and concerns outside of board meetings. • Serves as a nonexclusive conduit (to the CEO) of views, concerns, and issues of the independent directors.	• Facilitates discussion among the independent directors on key issues and concerns outside of board meetings. • Serves as a nonexclusive conduit (to the CEO) of views, concerns, and issues of the independent directors.
External Stakeholders	• Represents the organization when interacting with external stakeholders and employees.	• Typically has no role in representing the organization to external stakeholders. Some boards, however, occasionally ask their lead director to participate in meetings with key institutional investors.	• Can represent the organization when interacting with external stakeholders and employees at the discretion of the board of directors.
Company Operations	• Leads company operations. • Officers and employees report to him or her.	• Has no role in company operations. • Officers and employees report to CEO, not to him or her.	• Has no role in company operations. • Officers and employees report to CEO, not to him or her.

Source: Board Leadership—Report of the NACD Blue Ribbon Commission.

integrity, and interest among the directors and management in the boardroom. Another great tool for strengthening boardroom leadership is consistent education opportunities for all members of the board, with a special focus on the board chair and those leading the committees of the board. Also, a formal orientation program for all new board members and special education opportunities for those elected to be new committee chairs can strengthen the overall work of the board.

GOVERNANCE EVALUATIONS AND IMPROVEMENT

Governance has been around essentially as long as organizations have, but corporate failures in recent decades have pushed governance into the spotlight. Companies of different sizes and shapes, and with different cultures, may approach governance differently. But in any case, governance systems should be evaluated and there may be some bright-line rules or recommendations that can help all organizations to know if they are approaching leadership correctly.

Most companies have governance structures in place which conform to the growing list of regulations and guidelines, some domestic and some international. But an effective governance system should go beyond the minimum requirement of satisfying regulations. Governance structures must adapt as organizations and their environments change. Successful organizations ensure that they meet regulatory requirements, periodically evaluate results of their governance practices, and benchmark their governance practices against competitors and other companies with similarities.

A committee for the Professional Accountants in Business (PAIB) of the International Federation of Accountants (IFAC) has developed or collected principles that represent good practices for evaluating and improving governance and meeting governance goals, which include the following among others:

▶ The creation and optimization of sustainable stakeholder value should be the objective of governance.

▶ The governing body should establish a set of fundamental values by which the organization operates. All those participating in governance should embrace these fundamental values.

▶ The governing body should understand the organization's business model, its operating environment, and how sustainable stakeholder value is created and optimized.

▶ The governing body should periodically measure and evaluate the organization's strategic direction and business operations, and follow up with appropriate actions to ensure appropriate progress and continued alignment with objectives.

▶ The governing body should ensure that reasonable demands from stakeholders for information are met, and that the information provided is relevant, understandable, and reliable.[7]

It is vital that organizations measure their results and see how they are progressing against their objectives, and also that directors be held accountable for delivering value. Setting milestones and tangible goals will help with this process. Regular evaluation of governance structure should measure the system's effectiveness and search for methods of improvement. Boards should also be given the opportunity to evaluate themselves, as shown in Figure 6.3.

Not everyone believes that formal board evaluations are useful, however. Philip "Phil" A. Laskawy, former CEO of Ernst & Young and chairman of Fannie Mae, drew applause at a National Association of Corporate Directors (NACD) conference when he called board evaluations a waste of time.[8] Critics of board evaluations argue that little attention is paid to the process, with directors just

FIGURE 6.3 A Board's Self-Evaluation

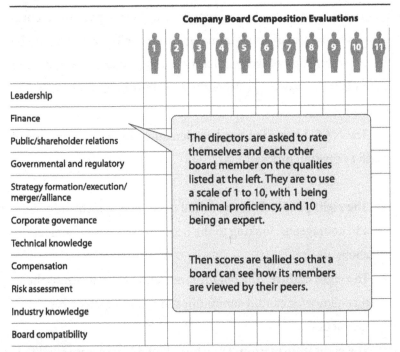

Some boards survey their members about fellow members in an effort to evaluate the qualities the board has as a whole.

Source: NACD Board Advisory Services.

ticking boxes—usually ones representing high scores for themselves or others reviewed. Many believe this is done for no other reason than to satisfy the New York Stock Exchange (NYSE) requirements for annual self-evaluations.[9]

Any evaluation process is going to have problems, but an alternative to the box-checking approach is to have directors sit down with a lead director or governance committee chair and discuss his or her performance and the performance of other specific directors. While there is the potential for more complete responses using this process, there is also the potential that board members will use less candor when speaking to someone face-to-face, especially in comparison to the use of anonymous written questionnaires. It may be that a combination of written questionnaires, interviews, and other methods is the way to go, depending on personnel and boardroom atmospherics.

The NACD has cited five key elements for having a successful board evaluation process:

1. **The right people.** Directors need to be independent-minded and courageous, looking to the best interests of shareholders above all else.
2. **The right culture.** The boardroom should have an atmosphere that allows for candid communications and constructive interaction.
3. **The right information.** Directors should have access to all the information they need to make informed decisions.
4. **The right process.** To evaluate itself, the board must know its goals and objectives and then find a way to measure how it is meeting those goals and objectives.
5. **The right follow-through.** The board must take appropriate corrective or constructive action on the results of the evaluations.[10]

A board should not view an evaluation as simply a mandated chore, but a way to improve performance and lead to an increase in shareholder value. It should be a dynamic process that at least has the potential to provide critical information to or about the board, such as whether the board is in need of another director with a unique skill set or whether committee performance could be

Best Practices and Transparency in Action: History, Values, and Governance Policies at Tenet

Model of Transparency with Key Governance Tools.

FIGURE 6.4 Corporate Governance at Tenet

Tenet's website lists the number of independent directors and financial experts on the audit committee, and answers questions about its governance and accountability.

- Annual board elections, and directors elected by the vote of a majority of votes cast in uncontested elections.

- The following committees are independent: The Audit Committee, the Compensation Committee, the Nominating and Corporate Governance Committee, and the Quality, Compliance & Ethics Committee.

- Number of financial experts on the Audit Committee is stated.

- There is a description of responsibilities for the *independent* chairman.

Corporate Governance

At Tenet Healthcare Corporation, we believe that sound principles of corporate governance serve the best interests of our shareholders and our other constituents, including patients, physicians, employees, suppliers and communities. We manage our business with integrity and the highest ethical standards, and we operate with transparency by measuring and communicating our results consistently.

We are committed to continually evolving and adopting appropriate corporate governance best practices. Please see our Corporate Governance Principles for additional information.

Board of Directors

Tenet's Board of Directors is elected by the company's shareholders to oversee management and to assure that the long-term interests of the shareholders are being served.

2013 Fact Sheet

Size of Board	9
Number of Independent Directors	8
Annual Board Elections	Yes
Directors Elected by the Vote of a Majority of Votes Cast in Uncontested Elections	Yes
Annual Review of Independence of Board	Yes
Separate Independent Chairman and CEO	Yes
Independent Audit Committee	Yes
Independent Compensation Committee	Yes
Independent Nominating and Corporate Governance Committee	Yes
Independent Quality, Compliance & Ethics Committee	Yes
Charters for Board Committees	Yes
Number of Audit Committee Financial Experts	3
Corporate Governance Principles Approved by the Board	Yes
Independent Chairman Description of Responsibilities	Yes
Compensation Committee Consultant Independence Policy	Yes
Director and Executive Officer Stock Ownership Guidelines	Yes
Number of Board Meetings Held or Scheduled	18
Independent Directors Meet Without Management Present	Yes
Annual Board Self-Evaluation Required	Yes
Key Committee Self-Evaluations Required	Yes
Annual Equity Grant to Non-Employee Directors	Yes
Board Orientation/Education Program	Yes
Corporate Compliance Program	Yes
Disclosure Committee for Financial Reporting	Yes

Tenet Healthcare Corporation is a superb example of a public company striving to use transparency and best practices in corporate governance (see Figure 6.4).

(Continued)

Incorporated in Nevada in 1975, Tenet Healthcare Corporation operates 78 hospitals, 183 outpatient centers, and Conifer Health Solutions, which provides business process solutions to more than 700 hospitals and other clients nationwide, as of the end of 2013. Tenet is now headquartered in downtown Dallas.

Tenet has more than 100,000 employees and has more than $11 billion in net operating revenues.[11] Tenet's mission "is to improve the quality of life of every patient who enters our doors," and the company is guided by five "core values"— quality, integrity, service, innovation, and transparency.[12]

Tenet leadership believes "that sound principles of corporate governance serve the best interests of our shareholders and our other constituents, including patients, physicians, employees, suppliers, and communities," and many of those principles are shared on Tenet's website—a testament to their dedication to one of their core values, transparency.[13]

Tenet lists its board of directors, which includes former Florida Governor Jeb Bush, and provides detailed descriptions of each director.[14] The website also lists the number of independent directors and financial experts on the audit committee, and answers to questions such as whether Tenet has an independent compensation committee (yes), whether it has annual board elections (yes), and whether annual self-evaluations are required for board members (yes).[15]

Tenet states that its board members must make a significant time commitment to the company and participate in continuing education programs.[16] Further, Tenet is committed to having an engaged, active board, and has a "Nominating and Corporate Governance Committee" that each year carefully considers each director's qualifications and contributions to the board.[17]

Since 2003, Tenet's independent directors have designated an independent, nonemployee director as chairman of the board.[18] In the event that a member of management is named chairman, the independent members of the board must designate an independent director as "lead director" for certain purposes, including facilitating information flow between the directors and the chairman.[19]

As a further matter of transparency, anyone who has a concern about Tenet's conduct, including accounting or auditing issues, may communicate that concern, confidentially or anonymously, to the Audit Committee by calling Tenet's "Ethics Action Line."[20]

improved. Other aspects of the board that may be improved by a strong evaluation process include: board leadership, meetings and agendas, the board/management relationship, and communication and board objectives.

BOARD AND CEO SUCCESSION PLANNING TODAY

Executive succession planning is the process by which the board of directors attempts to ensure that executives, in particular, chief executive officers (CEOs), have capable and willing replacements and that the transition to a new CEO goes smoothly. Changing CEOs can cause significant disruption to a company, both positive and negative, and yet almost half of U.S. companies with $500 million in revenue have no meaningful succession plan[21] and on average boards spend only two hours per year on CEO succession planning.[22] Succession problems at public companies such as Apple and Bank of America have rightfully brought the issue to the forefront for shareholders.

Successful companies have a plan in place for grooming and/ or selecting succession candidates, who may succeed as part of a planned succession or because of an unplanned CEO exit. A smooth transition is integral to:

- Maintaining a good CEO–board relationship
- Maintaining the confidence of investors, customers, and business partners
- Sustaining a company's success

Boards should have an idea of when the tenure of their CEOs will naturally run their course, but they should also have an emergency plan in place.

Because of how important it is that the transition goes well, the board of directors must make implementation of an effective succession plan a priority, although it may seem that there are more tangible issues at hand. Continuous succession planning, undertaken even during prosperous times, helps ease the stress of succession that may occur when the company is in dire straits.

John Hanson, the former CEO of Joy Global, stated the importance of ongoing succession planning as follows: "The board has to understand, not just explicitly, but intuitively, that CEO succession is its most critical responsibility. If the board truly does understand that instinctively, then it will constantly be working the succession issue and it will always see the process in the context of a continuum."[23]

Good succession planning is intended to ensure that the next CEO is a good one, but it also has beneficial by-products, including:

- Improving the communication and overall relationship between the board and senior management through regular correspondence about succession candidates.
- Improving management quality throughout the company by recognizing strategic needs at the top of the firm and training managers in accordance with firm goals.

Renowned business consultant Ram Charan has cited three actions companies should take to minimize succession problems and pitfalls:

- Ensure that there is a deep pool of qualified succession candidates.
- Have an updated succession plan and thought process for making decisions about candidates.
- If directors are considering outside candidates, they should be exacting and informed and not simply rely on outside recruiters.[24]

Nearly 40 percent of Fortune 1000 companies are run by CEOs who were recruited from outside of the company.[25] While the practice is fairly routine, one downside is that outsiders don't have the same familiarity with the ins and outs of the company that someone groomed from within may have. As a result, some of the recruited CEOs do not last as long as insider successors. That so many companies are being led by outsiders may also be an indictment of these companies' ability to develop leadership talent. Finally, outsiders tend to come with much higher price tags than those promoted from within.

Charan finds that promoting insiders has its own set of problems, including:

▶ The hiring of "known quantities" who may sail through a lax due-diligence process.
▶ Promoting individuals from functional areas who may not be suited for leading an entire business.
▶ If the outgoing CEO did an extremely poor job, the reputation of internal candidates may be affected negatively by association.[26]

Executive search and leadership consulting firm Spencer Stuart conducted a study of CEO transitions in the mid- to late-2000s to see which types of CEOs produced the best results (e.g., insiders, outsiders, etc.). The study found that insiders and outsiders performed about the same,[27] and neither of which performed as well as when board members were made CEO.[28] The group that performed the worst was titled "insider-outsiders"—outsiders who were brought in to take over a non-CEO position but then were later made CEO.[29] A possible explanation for this is that the outsider is made to audition for the CEO role and in appeasing the current CEO merely becomes his or her duplicate.

Neither insiders, outsiders, nor any other category of individuals make perfect successors, which demonstrates the basic problem: finding a CEO successor is hard. Charan estimates that a corporation with 70,000 employees may have five strong internal candidates for CEO— as he puts it, "It takes a ton of ore to produce an ounce of gold."[30] Additionally, realistic candidates need to be groomed early, and so those candidates need to be recognized early—something that is easier said than done. Candidates must need to be *identified* at an early age and then *nurtured* through training and valuable experience.

Once a leading candidate is recognized, a planned transition may begin by slowly moving the prospective CEO into the job in stages or into a different executive position such as chief financial officer (CFO) while retaining the ability to reverse course if things don't work out. Scholars have stated that there are five stages to successful CEO transition:

1. **Candidate flight test.** The candidate is assessed performing CEO or similar tasks.
2. **Designation as CEO.** The CEO is chosen by the board.
3. **Official announcement.** The CEO is announced to the public.
4. **Overlap.** The incoming and outgoing CEOs work together so that the new CEO is acclimated to the job.
5. **Freshman year.** The new CEO takes over and continues to be advised and assessed by the board.[31]

To do their part, boards must dedicate sufficient time and resources to address succession planning. They need to do their own due diligence and not pass their responsibilities on to third-party recruiters. Boards have a fiduciary duty to contemplate and prepare for major risks the company faces, including the loss of a CEO. This duty requires boards to act in good faith, to act with diligence, and to act in the best interests of the company.

Recruiters can be a useful tool for busy boards that may not have strong human resources abilities, but they should not simply be a crutch for boards. Recruiters can help boards identify needs and candidates, and can provide a fresh perspective to boards prone to tunnel vision. At the same time, recruiters do not know a company's business nearly as well the board does and the intricacies of the company must come into play when looking for a new leader.

In addition to making plans for CEO succession, boards should have a succession plan in place for directors. Annual evaluations and renominations should examine each director's engagement and performance. Boards should also consider mechanisms such as age and term limits in order to ensure some level of change.

In summary, succession planning needs to start early, not simply when it becomes clear that the current CEO is obviously on his or her way out. A related way to ease the burdens of succession planning is to focus on developing talent and building a reserve of possible leaders. Assuming the board moves toward fulfilling these responsibilities, transition periods—even those involving sudden CEO departures—can be made as painless as possible.

CASE STUDY: DIRECTORS WHO MADE A DIFFERENCE AT FORD MOTOR COMPANY

William Clay Ford, Jr., Executive Chairman and Chairman of the Board, was direct with his message in the 2006 Ford Motor Company Annual Report:

> After a difficult year in 2006, Ford Motor Company stands at a pivotal crossroad. In the face of fierce global competition,

we are taking dramatic and sometimes painful steps to transform our business. We have improved our cost structure, raised our quality, obtained financing, and refilled our product pipeline with exciting new vehicles.

Alan Mulally, our new president and CEO, is an engineer who is passionate about customers and knows how to win in a global market. . . .

We are taking actions to reduce our operating costs and realign our capacity to reflect the realities of the market. . . .

The ongoing success of Ford Motor Company is my life's work. I want us to be the company that makes a difference in people's lives. . . . To do that we must deliver desirable products with a competitive cost structure and a sustainable business model.

We are taking major steps to ensure that we succeed at these fundamentals, as well as our larger mission. I am confident in our team and in our plan. And I am more determined than ever to build a great Ford Motor Company for the next 100 years and beyond.[32]

Alan Mulally, new president and CEO, was equally frank with his words in his first Annual Report, "Ford Motor Company's results in 2006 were unacceptable. We had a full-year net loss of $12.6 billion, or $6.72 per share."[33]

It is 2013. The transformation of Ford is taking its well-deserved place as perhaps the greatest corporate turnaround ever in U.S. history. In 2006, the picture was bleak and the future of Ford was in doubt. Losses hit bottom in 2008 at $14.6 billion. By 2011, Ford completed its third year in a row of improved annual operating profits and announced the reinstatement of paying quarterly dividends for the first time in years. The good news continues unabated.

So how did Ford reinvent itself, avoid Chapter 11 bankruptcy like its competitors GM and Chrysler, and survive the worst economic slump of the auto industry in decades? And of greatest interest to me as a person committed to good governance, did the board of directors play a role in the survival and success of Ford?

Often, the theory of good corporate governance fails to translate into success and positive results. The history of corporations and governance is replete with numerous notable failures in governance including Enron, WorldCom, The Walt Disney Company, and Hewlett-Packard to name a few.

I wondered if the board did play a role in the transformation at Ford, what specific role they played? To answer my questions on the role of the board in the Ford transformation, I researched the records, studied the publications, and had the good fortune to connect with some of the players around the table as events unfolded.

Did the board of directors have a role and make a difference in the transformation at Ford in 2006? I believe they did and here is how.

The record and interviews show that the Ford board did indeed play a key role in the success of Ford. According to presiding director of Ford in 2006 Irvine O. Hockaday, Jr., and others[34]:

► The Ford board played a key role in helping William Clay Ford, Jr., find, engage, and hire the right President and CEO, Alan R. Mulally.

Past efforts to hire outsiders at Ford had not worked well. Finding a top CEO is a delicate matter, especially in a family-dominated business like Ford. For reasons of confidentiality and against conventional wisdom, the board in concert with then CEO William Ford, Jr., decided not to use a professional search firm, and elected to do the risky heavy lifting of finding, engaging, and hiring the next CEO. The risk paid off.

The board personally handled and completed the search. William Ford, Jr., resigned as CEO and hired a Boeing engineer with no auto experience, Alan Mulally, to be CEO on the recommendation of the board.

Alan Mulally is widely credited with leading a dramatic turnaround. William Ford, Jr., as executive chairman, and the Ford board worked well together as a group and in supporting this outstanding CEO.

▶ A core group of dedicated directors stood by the company, even in its darkest hour.

Leadership is a foul-weather job. Reputations are important. At times, even experienced directors weigh their personal reputations against their corporate responsibilities as directors. Indeed, the heat at Ford reached the point where several prominent directors resigned for various personal or professional reasons. Fortunately, a core group of directors committed to stay the course and fought the good fight.

▶ The board supported risky strategic decisions like "bet the farm" financing in December 2006 to obtain $23.5 billion of new liquidity, ignored the tempting options of federal bailouts or bankruptcy, and supported difficult decisions like the elimination of all dividends for many years. A bold financing plan was no easy decision during a dramatic market downturn and time of financial stress.

The board worked with management to support an aggressive finance plan that provided essential liquidity.

Conventional wisdom said GM and Chrysler would gain enormous competitive advantage in costs and pricing if Ford did not take bailouts or bankruptcy. The board supported Ford being the one company in the U.S. auto industry not taking direct government aid and built on this as a point of distinction and strength.

Ford Motor Company is a real-life rare example of dual-class stock structures in a public company. The board worked with the Ford family owners to eliminate all cash dividends for years when important to the future of the company. This cooperative working relationship on dividends was vital to the financing plan.

The board invested the time and work to truly become a cohesive board over the long term. Often, boards work well together on the surface. It takes time, energy, and hard work for a board to develop into a truly cohesive group. Learning to disagree agreeably takes a special talent. And while attending to rules and regulations is important board work, how board members work together makes for boards that are truly cohesive and can achieve success together over the long term. Ford achieved a highly cohesive board that worked well with the management team as it implemented its successful turnaround.

There is strong evidence that Ford Motor Company from 2006 to 2013 was fortunate to have a board of directors that worked collaboratively with management, became a cohesive useful group, and was a board that got it right.

Please consider the following three discussion points.

Discussion Point 1: Is the board useful?

Corporate boards, especially those at the prominent public company level, can be viewed as a special group operating in rarefied
air. The story goes that with some corporate boards, posing the
most negative view possible: "The board shows up infrequently, has
a good meal, jumps management through the hoops, leaves, comes
back and does it again. And the directors receive a fine fee to boot."

- ▶ The challenge for boards is to be useful. In what ways do you
  think the Ford board was useful in this reality-based Case
  Study?
- ▶ Is it best for a board to "stay at arm's length" from the CEO or
  can the board "jump into an active working partnership" with
  the CEO?

Discussion Point 2: Big ego or humble service, what works best?

CEOs and leaders can have strong personalities and big egos. They
can also pursue humble servant leader attitudes. Some CEOs insist
on being both CEO and board chair, while other CEOs work with
a separate independent board chair. What are your thoughts on the
following scenarios with Ford Motor Company?

- ▶ Chairman and CEO William C. Ford, Jr., when seeking a
  new CEO was perfectly willing to hand off both the chairman and CEO roles for the right candidate. What are your
  thoughts? Candidate Alan Mulally, when advised that the

combined chairman and CEO role would be available for the right candidate, immediately stated that if offered the CEO role he would insist that William C. Ford, Jr., stay on in the chairman of the board role at Ford. What are your thoughts?

Discussion Point 3: Is the board cohesive?

What are your thoughts on building a cohesive board?

- What evidence do you see of a cohesive board at Ford?
- In what ways do you think boards can become more cohesive?
- Can you give examples of success or failure with a company building a cohesive board?

Chapter 7

ACTIVIST SHAREHOLDERS AND THEIR ROLE IN GOVERNANCE

Rising shareholder activism at public companies in recent years has drawn an unusual amount of attention from the media, public company boards, and their executives. If it continues, and it almost surely will, it holds the potential to change life in the corporate boardroom. More activist shareholders are churning the waters and some are actually taking seats at the boardroom table. As a result, directors are under pressure to hear a wider range of views than just the opinions from management and the more conventional group of directors.

Public company shareholder activism boils down to someone believing he or she has a better idea as to the value of a company and its stock. More specifically, this someone thinks he or she can do a better job than the current management and board in getting the stock market to recognize a company's value on an accelerated timeline. Activist shareholders typically express their belief by purchasing a comparatively large block of a company's shares of stock and then actively seeking to make things happen in the company.

Notable activist shareholders in the decade of 2003 to 2013 include Carl Icahn of Icahn Enterprises LP, William "Bill" Ackman of Pershing Square Capital Management, LP, and Daniel S. Loeb of Third Point LLC. Some of the more prominent shareholder battles these activists waged took on no less than Apple Inc., Sony Corporation, and Dell Inc. Other major activist battles of the decade involved J. C. Penney Company Inc. (JCPenney), Herbalife Ltd., Target Corporation, Borders Group, Inc., and Chesapeake Energy Corporation.

There are several overarching reasons for why attention should be given to activist shareholders and how the concepts apply to good governance overall:

▸ Activist shareholders look to gain attention at the top of the organization by communicating with the board of directors. Indeed, activists regularly seek to "claim" one or more seats at the boardroom table when taking on companies. As we reviewed early with governance, shareholders elect directors and directors oversee management. Thus, boards have a vital role in the direction of a company. Activists want to be heard and have a vote. Who doesn't?

▸ Related to directors overseeing the management of a company is a personal observation from extensive work in governance. When companies are thriving, you most often find a visionary leader and a board of directors that is doing its job. Conversely, I have observed that when companies are failing, almost inevitably there is a board of directors that has failed in some aspect of its governance responsibilities. Thus, my use of the statement *"When it is not working at the top, it is usually not working anywhere in the company"* is my recognition that governance really matters in both basic and profound ways. Basic ways, like hiring the right CEO. Profound ways, like a board having a serious grasp on the company's strategy and utilizing modern tools to insure good governance, such as objective board and director self-assessments.

▶ Activist shareholders in the years 2010 to 2014 have gained a new momentum and place at the table with the boards and executives of many of the public companies they pursue and make investments in. Boards and management teams are engaging at a far more active level with all shareholders, and that is especially true when it comes to many of the sophisticated activist shareholder groups that target companies today. As we saw with Carl Icahn making a large investment in Apple, CEO Tim Cook took the time to meet with Icahn as a large investor representing a number of like-minded investors.

WHY DO ACTIVIST SHAREHOLDERS TAKE ON PUBLIC COMPANIES?

Activist shareholders seek to make extraordinary financial returns for their investors. Last year Carl Icahn told *Forbes* that the stock performance for his company Icahn Enterprises, which focuses on activism, showed a return of 1,122 percent during the same period the Standard & Poor's 500 (S&P 500) returned 46 percent and the Dow Jones Industrial Average (DJIA) returned 85 percent.[1]

Icahn operates as a public company. Many activist shareholders are private-equity firms or private investors of extreme wealth known for taking big risks and seeking big returns. Often, the partner investors in the private equity funds are wealthy persons, large pension funds, and large university or foundation endowments like the Harvard Endowment, which often invest up to 20 percent of their billions in assets with private equity funds. These private-equity firms seek to purchase some or all of the shares in an *undervalued* company stock with the intent to get control. They then force the board and management to make positive changes to the company's operations, thereby creating a terrific return on investment.

Leon Black's Apollo Global Management LLC took a gamble with billions to buy and take a public company group of real estate brokerages private in 2007 at the start of the worst housing crash since the Great Depression. From 2008 until 2011, that private company, Realogy Holdings Corp., was often reported to be on the verge of bankruptcy and saw its number of offices shrink from 1,500 to 1,100. Realogy cut 5,000 jobs, a third of its workforce.

By October 2012, Realogy went public again listing on the New York Stock Exchange (NYSE) with a $1.2 billion initial public offering (IPO), according to the *Wall Street Journal*. That provided Black's Apollo a total return of almost double the $1.3 billion invested after many years of hard work. It was a nice return, but short of the typical four times or more in gains that private-equity firms often aim for with buyouts.

Big risks for big returns is the driving force for most activist shareholders, though some espouse more altruistic reasons, like companies becoming more productive and creating more jobs. And like most investments, the risk of big losses is ever present.

In 2013, long-time private-equity shareholder activist investor William "Bill" Ackman, renowned for years for making big bets for big returns, ran into a buzzsaw with two of his public company investments in J. C. Penney Company and Herbalife Ltd. The two companies handed his investment firm almost a billion dollars in losses, along with some unusually bruising public boardroom fights. "Clearly, retail has not been our strong suit, and this is duly noted," Ackman noted in a summary letter to investors, which was quoted in the *Wall Street Journal*.[2]

Dueling Activists and Short Selling Stocks

William Ackman's Herbalife bet highlights two fascinating details of the rough and tumble high stakes world of activist shareholder investing—dueling activists and short selling of stocks. Often activists will use short selling to bet on a stock that is falling in price. Critics regularly claim short sellers may be improperly acting to drive a stock price down, like talking poorly in public about a stock. And activists regularly take opposing bets with target companies, making separate public cases why the same stock will soar or crash in the months ahead.

In the case of Herbalife Ltd., Ackman went to the press in December 2012 with his assertions that Herbalife, as a multilevel marketing company selling nutrition products, was nothing more than a classic pyramid scheme that regulators including the Securities and Exchange Commission (SEC) and states attorneys general would do well to investigate and shut down. Ackman claimed Herbalife's distributors make their money from enrolling new recruits to sell the product rather than from the sale of product, a pyramid plan sure to fail sooner than later.

Ackman started buying a short position of Herbalife shares in the $33 price range, with the stock dropping some 25 percent in days immediately following his allegations. Well-known investors Carl Icahn, George Soros, and William P. Stiritz took the position over the following months that Herbalife was a legitimate business and greatly undervalued, and they piled into the stock. A year after Ackman's initial claims, the stock price had increased 130 percent.

Based on the December 2013 price of the stock, Svea Herbst-Bayliss of Reuters wrote: "The founder of Pershing Square Capital Management has seen the value of his $1 billion short play against Herbalife lose nearly three-quarters of a billion dollars in 2013, making it one of the 10-year-old fund's riskiest bets."[3]

What Is the Impact of Activists on Public Company Boards and Management?

The impact of activists on public company boards and management ultimately depends on the quality and merits of the activist's case for recommended changes at the targeted company. The historical record is wide-ranging indeed. The impact can range from outright rejection of the activist's ideas, to no noticeable change, to the company selectively pursuing strategic or operational changes suggested by the activist, to directors being added or removed, to CEO changes, to companies being taken private or sold, and more. Of course what the activists are looking for is simply this: enhanced value and return on investment (ROI).

From my perspective, there is great value to studying, in detail, the actions of activist shareholders. Whether you love them or hate them, activists most always shine a spotlight on some of the most interesting companies of our times and many of their related strategic, operational, financial, and governance issues.

Ralph Whitworth has run Relational Investors LLC since 1996, a privately owned asset management firm and investment advisor registered with the U.S. Securities and Exchange Commission (SEC). Relational Investors serves some of the largest pension funds in the world and describes its work as seeking to "produce superior returns" by influencing the direction of its portfolio companies. While the mission statement does not use the word "activist," it is revealing:

> Relational invests in and strives to create long-term growth in publicly traded, underperforming companies that it believes are undervalued in the marketplace. Through intense and focused research, Relational develops an engagement plan to unlock value in its portfolio companies. The Firm seeks to engage the management, board of directors, and shareholders of a portfolio company in a productive dialogue designed to build a consensus for positive change to improve shareholder value.[4]

Whitworth's work over the years has come to focus intensely on corporate governance, as highlighted in a rare 2008 *Financial Times* interview by Francesco Guerrera and James Politi:

> "We don't go and argue over strategy and the business plan," Whitworth told the reporters.
>
> Instead, Mr. Whitworth picks fights with companies where he considers boards are in thrall to their chief executive and are making poor decisions, be it on executive compensation, acquisitions, or corporate malfeasance.

By entering the fray and forcing companies to change their ways, often from the inside as a board member, Mr. Whitworth believes it can quickly add value for itself and other shareholders. The approach seems to have worked.[5]

Whitworth has served on 11 boards, helping oust CEOs like Robert Nardelli of The Home Depot and Gary Forsee of Sprint Nextel Corporation. In April 2013, Whitworth was named interim chairman for Hewlett-Packard, having been a director since 2011.[6]

Activist War Stories and Board Battles

Here we will review Carl Icahn and O. Mason Hawkins in the context of events involving these investors and well-known corporate icons Apple Inc., Chesapeake Energy Corporation, and Dell Inc. My focus here will be to highlight key methods and motivations of activist shareholders, rather than to give too many details of any particular case. Are the activists modern-day Robin Hoods doing good works for all shareholders? Are the board members of target companies working hard at good governance or villains neglecting their duties? Or is it a far more complex matter in a dynamically changing market?

After sharing these cases, I will close with key thoughts on how to respond when activist investors knock on the door. And knock they almost certainly will at a company known to you.

Apple Inc. and Carl Icahn

Billionaire activist investor Carl Icahn thought Apple shares were seriously undervalued in August 2013 and quickly bought up some

$2.5 billion in shares. He met with CEO Tim Cook in September 2013 to encourage a $150 billion share buyback and filed a shareholder proposal with the company for its annual shareholders' meeting calling for that course of action. Icahn and other investors were captivated with Apple's cash balance approaching $150 billion.

In Figure 7.1, you will find a snippet of Icahn's letter of October 24, 2013 to CEO Tim Cook with his key thoughts including: the logic of the buyback, their common belief that the shares are undervalued, and Icahn's suggestion that Apple's board needs a director with a track record as an investment professional.

I would call this a remarkably friendly approach for an activist with a long record of aggressive proxy battles and the like over many decades. The fact that Tim Cook met with Icahn fits with the current trend of CEOs and boards meeting with activists to hear what they have to say.

Icahn's early friendly approach is encouraging to see. Even so, he has strong opinions on the need for continued governance reform, in general, and apart from Apple. His philosophy is expressed here from his brief letter of welcome to those who joined his website platform known as "Shareholders' Square Table" in 2013:

Dear Member,

Thank you for joining the Shareholders' Square Table and becoming part of an important campaign for Corporate Democracy.

The public companies in this country suffer from poor corporate governance. Among many other problems, poor corporate governance allows for a growing disparity in income best reflected by CEOs of public companies earning

FIGURE 7.1 Shareholders Taking a Stand

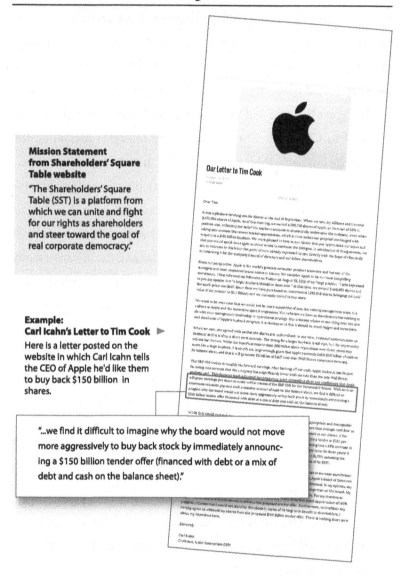

Mission Statement from Shareholders' Square Table website

"The Shareholders' Square Table (SST) is a platform from which we can unite and fight for our rights as shareholders and steer toward the goal of real corporate democracy."

Example: Carl Icahn's Letter to Tim Cook ▷

Here is a letter posted on the website in which Carl Icahn tells the CEO of Apple he'd like them to buy back $150 billion in shares.

"...we find it difficult to imagine why the board would not move more aggressively to buy back stock by immediately announcing a $150 billion tender offer (financed with debt or a mix of debt and cash on the balance sheet)."

One example of shareholders engaging actively in dialogue with companies about their governance is Carl Icahn's group, Shareholders' Square Table.

as much as 700 times the wages of an average employee. Even though these companies often underperform, the Board of Directors continues to overpay the CEO because poor corporate governance allows for a dramatic and universal lack of accountability. This is a huge problem for shareholders, and for our economy. As shareholders, the time has come for us to stand together and make a change. I intend for the Shareholders' Square Table to be a platform enabling us to do this together.

Sincerely,

Carl Icahn[7]

This Letter of Welcome by Icahn touches on three of the most common complaints or causes you regularly hear about corporate boards and their executives from activist shareholders in their takeover efforts:

- Unrealistic and unjustified CEO compensation
- Lack of accountability for executives by their boards
- Poor decisions by executives and boards

The complaint about overpaid CEO compensation is the same one we heard earlier from Warren Buffett. Complaints on high CEO compensation is interesting to me in that successful activist shareholders and private equity managers are renowned for their enormous paychecks, some of the largest on Wall Street. Having studied activist shareholders over the years, I believe their replies would be the same as Warren Buffett's, with the view that we have no problem with enormous pay packages when the CEO creates enormous value for the shareholders as well. We object to CEOs who have destroyed shareholder value with poor decisions by the CEO and the board.

Returning to Icahn's initial friendly approach with Apple Inc., his letter of October 24, 2013, reflects terrific admiration and support:

". . . We want to be very clear that we could not be more supportive of you, the existing management team, the culture of Apple and the innovative spirit it engenders. This criticism we have as shareholders has nothing to do with your management leadership or operational strategy. Our criticism relates to one thing only: the size and time frame of Apple's buyback program. It is obvious to us that it should be much bigger and immediate."[8]

The letter goes on to suggest point blank an example of classic activist financial engineering:

". . . As we proposed at our dinner, if the company decided to borrow the full $150 billion at a 3% interest rate to commence a tender at $525 per share, the result would be an immediate 33% boost to earnings per share, translating into a 33% increase in the value of the shares, which significantly assumes no multiple expansion."[9]

Apple had responded politely that the prior board-approved $60 billion repurchase would continue and would consider added changes in the future. Classic reasons to object to the buyback would include:

- ► A need to have cash for major acquisitions in an intensely competitive environment.
- ► The desire to pay dividends with the cash.
- ► The need for major cash reserves for the long haul in a rocky marketplace.

It has also been suggested by others, like Henry Blodget of *Business Insider,* that there is a special challenge in that "Apple's cash balance is mostly stored overseas, so Apple can't use the cash to buy back the $150 billion of stock without paying huge taxes on the 'repatriation.' Thus Icahn's suggestion that the company borrow it."[10]

O. Mason Hawkins

O. Mason Hawkins could be called the reluctant activist shareholder. He is chairman and CEO of Southeastern Asset Management, Inc., an independent global money manager. Southeastern invests in under-valued securities for clients worldwide. It has operated since 1975 through its family of funds called the Longleaf Partners Funds.[11]

As explained in the "Letter To Our Shareholders" in the Longleaf Partners Funds' first quarter report of 2013, "Activism' is not part of our normal process, nor is it our preferred work."[12] Their invest-ment approach and report explains that when Longleaf evaluates a stock it carefully assesses "management partners." When Longleaf invests in a stock that ends up failing, most of the time it simply exits the position by selling the stock. Conversely, a very clear case is given for becoming active when the undervaluation relates to the management partners:

"When the company's underlying assets remain strong, the stock's undervaluation is compelling, and the primary 'fix' relates to people, we will generally become active if we believe we have good odds of successfully improving our clients' outcome.

". . . in the last twenty years, we have owned 242 U.S. names and filed just twenty-five 13D's."[13] This implies that Longleaf has been active with 13D filings in about 10 percent of their holdings over the years.

"Fighting for our clients has been worth the effort. In over three-fourths of the cases where we filed 13D's, the stock price rose from the filing point through our holding period."[14]

"Standing up for our clients via activism has been worthwhile."[15]

O. Mason Hawkins and Chesapeake Energy Corporation

Chesapeake Energy Corporation highlights a holding where Southeastern Asset Management, Inc., was actively engaged in a stock holding that it had invested in over many years. Ultimately, activism led by Southeastern resulted in profound changes in governance at Chesapeake.

Headquartered in Oklahoma City, Chesapeake was cofounded in 1989 by former CEO Aubrey McClendon and former president and COO Tom Ward to pursue natural gas exploration and production. The company grew at a spectacular rate and rapidly assembled large holdings of natural gas assets around the United States. The company completed an initial public offering (IPO) in 1993.

Southeastern was a staunch supporter of the controversial CEO McClendon for years. It became Chesapeake's largest shareholder, holding some 13 percent of the shares worth hundreds of millions of dollars. As late as December 2011, Southeastern was showing support for Chesapeake and McClendon.

When an activist shareholder's patience runs out, things move fast. By November 2012, Southeastern reported, in "The Letter To Our Shareholders" in its third quarter report of 2012, on some really dramatic changes to Chesapeake's governance:

". . . With pressure from Southeastern as well as Carl Icahn, Chesapeake replaced six of nine directors, split the CEO and chairman roles, and restructured board and CEO compensation. From the stock's low in May, the price has risen 39% following these

changes. Going forward, the directors, who collectively own meaningful shares, will seek to insure financial discipline in capital
expenditure and debt decisions."[16]

In this scenario, you will notice a number of the classic governance reforms and best practices. The new directors were all
independent, with no prior relationships to Chesapeake or its
CEO. Archie W. Dunham, former chairman of ConocoPhillips and
former CEO of Conoco, was named the new independent nonexecutive chairman. Dunham had no previous relationship with
Chesapeake and became the second chairman in Chesapeake's history. Also, CEO and board pay was restructured.[17]

Mention was made of Carl Icahn. Together he and Southeastern owned some 22 percent of the shares. By late January 2013,
reports of McClendon's exit as CEO surfaced, and he did in fact
retire in early April 2013.

By November 2013, just 18 months after making public its dis-
pleasure, Southeastern reported, in its third quarter report, on the
success of Chesapeake's new CEO and the impact of good management on its investments:

"The common theme in our strongest contributors in the quarter was that they illustrate the meaningful impact that good management can have. Our newly installed CEOs have shown quick
results. Doug Lawler at Chesapeake implemented significant cost
cuts, lowered capital spending, and sold noncore assets. . . . The
actions of these CEOs contributed meaningfully to our successful
quarter."[18]

Dell, O. Mason Hawkins, and Carl Icahn

Perhaps the most notable activist shareholder battle in recent history started in late 2012 with a highly publicized battle over Dell

Inc. The matter was finally put to rest when Michael Dell and the investment firm Silver Lake Partners lead a management buyout (MBO) and took the company private.

Here is what you would find if you access the Dell website and click the Investor tab:

Dell is now a private company. On September 12, 2013, Dell stockholders approved the proposal in which Michael Dell, Dell's founder, chairman and CEO, will acquire Dell in partnership with global technology investment firm Silver Lake Partners. The merger transaction closed on October 29, 2013, and the company has commenced the process to delist its common shares from the NASDAQ Stock Market. Per the merger agreement, Dell shareholders are entitled to receive $13.75 in cash, in addition to a special dividend of $0.13 per common share.

As a private company, we are going back to our roots, to the entrepreneurial spirit that made Dell one of the fastest growing, most successful companies in history. We're unleashing the creativity and confidence that have always been the hallmarks of our culture. We will be able to serve our customers with a single-minded purpose and drive the innovations that will change our world for the better.[19]

As with the case of Chesapeake Energy, O. Mason Hawkins and Longleaf Partners Funds of Southeastern Asset Management, Inc., had invested heavily in Dell for many years. As of December 2011, Dell was Longleaf's largest holding, representing 8.9 percent of the fund.[20]

Hawkins, through Longleaf Partners, was a long-term staunch supporter of both Dell and Michael Dell, even in the face of dramatic adverse changes taking place in the PC market for desktop and laptop computers. Hawkins, of the company Southeastern Asset Management, then the largest shareholder of Dell stock, was one of the first to suggest the idea of Dell going private in June 2012, according to reports.[21]

Michael Dell found a partner to take Dell private with an initial offer of $11.22 per share. Apparently the price was less than hoped for by some. Hawkins of Southeastern and Carl Icahn both went public with their case that the offered price was far below Dell's true value. Southeastern published a letter on February 8, 2012, providing its detailed financial analysis stating that Dell was worth $24 per share. Icahn also issued a number of letters to Dell's board and their special board committee evaluating matters related to the proposed "go-private transaction."

Michael Dell's negotiations with the special board committee played out over many months in 2013 like a world championship chess match, with a number of players involved. As reflected in the notice from the Dell website, in September 2013, Dell shareholders approved the go-private transaction for Dell at a price of $13.75 per share plus a special dividend.

Hawkins reported in Longleaf's 2013 third quarter report his disappointment with the Dell transaction as an MBO well below the value of Dell's free cash flow and assets.[22] It highlighted Southeastern's efforts as an activist to obtain a higher offer. In the end, his clients got a better outcome including a higher price per share.

Icahn posted an "Open Letter To Dell Stockholders," dated September 9, 2013, as a type of postmortem that I found most gracious all things considered.

Here are some of Icahn's thoughts from his "Open Letter":

I realize that some stockholders will be disappointed that we do not fight on, Icahn wrote. "Michael Dell/Silver Lake waged a hard fought battle and. . . the actions by Dell were within the Delaware law. We therefore congratulate Michael Dell and I intend to call him to wish him good luck (he may need it).[23]

Key Thoughts on How to Respond When the Activist Investor Knocks

- ► Be aware that shareholder activism is on the rise.
- ► Know your largest shareholders and keep up on large purchases.
- ► Know if you are a potential target in the eyes of activists.
- ► Know the activists and their unique approaches.
- ► Know that some of the classic legal and governance tools for defense from activists are out of favor, like classified boards and shareholder rights plans.
- ► Be prepared to respond to the typical activist request for board seats by having the CEO and board leaders ready to talk or listen, as appropriate.

> ▶ Be prepared to meet with the activist. Who from the board and management will take the meeting and what will your agenda be?
> ▶ Be as objective and as dispassionate as you can about any activist proposal. Seek expert advice and counsel, as needed.

IF IT IS NOT WORKING AT THE TOP

Related to the new momentum and recognition of activist shareholders that pursue public companies is the reality that many of these intense and often fast-moving activist shareholder engagements (or "attacks" as some call them) tend to focus very clearly and quickly on some of the most important governance and operating issues that public companies face on a current basis. With Carl Icahn and Apple Inc. we saw, within months, a very public debate on the pros and cons of Icahn's desire for Apple to quickly do a massive $150 billion share repurchase. Important governance voices like Institutional Shareholder Services Inc. (ISS) and CalPERS, the giant pension fund, weighed in on why Apple was wise to hold on to the pile of cash.[24]

ISS reported that "The board's latitude should not be constricted by a shareholder resolution that would micromanage the company's capital allocation process."[25] The report also praised Apple for making "good-faith efforts" to adopt more shareholder friendly policies.[26]

This tendency to focus very clearly and quickly on some of the most important governance and operating issues that public companies face on a current basis—this microscopic review—highlights in a very public way some of the most important governance trends and operating issues companies face today. And this does not just apply to public companies. While most of the activist shareholder battles take place with public companies, the governance concepts and operating issues addressed in the public company battles often set governance trends and operating ideas for companies of all types—public, private, and nonprofit, and even government entities at times.

One such activist shareholder battle, the Herbalife saga discussed earlier in the chapter, continued into its second year in early 2014. As the Federal Trade Commission (FTC) investigated hedge-fund manager Bill Ackman's claims that the company was a pyramid scheme, Carl Icahn had 3 more of his representatives named Herbalife board members—giving Icahn a total of 5 members of the 13-person board.[27]

Activists tend to find target companies that:

- May present an opportunity for a big return.
- Are undervalued, for whatever reasons.
- Could better unlock shareholder value.
- Have significant issues with board composition, leadership, or governance in general.

Activist tools include:

- Nomination of directors
- Bylaw amendments
- Press releases
- Demands for corporate records
- Letters to the board and/or shareholders

There are several steps a company can take if it believes it may be the subject of an activist campaign:

► Get to know the activist and its typical modus operandi.
► Assess the company's defenses and if they can be improved.
► Determine if and/or how the activist should be engaged, including by public comment.
► Play out possible scenarios.
► Seek expert advice and counsel, as needed.

Having a comprehensive "vulnerability assessment" in advance of any activist campaign may prevent a lot of headaches, if not the campaign in its entirety. Another approach, however, is for companies to think like activists and to know themselves the best governance operations and the best ways to unlock shareholder value.

Activist shareholders are increasingly well-prepared, well-funded, and well-advised. They approach situations and opportunities with an extraordinary understanding of the businesses they are seeking to alter or affect, and companies and their boards must therefore account and prepare for them.

Take note that it is not just activist shareholders that can place demands on boards for top performance. Bankers, creditors, disgruntled shareholders, employees, unions, attorneys general, and more can look over the shoulders of directors on a regular basis.

We wrap with a final case study from past years that is similar to the Herbalife situation in that it also involved a public company built on multilevel marketing sales. Pre-Paid Legal Services, Inc. had the Securities and Exchange Commission (SEC) looking over its shoulder and more. Let's see what governance trends and operating ideas you can bring to the boardroom table in your role as a public company director for Pre-Paid Legal Services, Inc.

CASE STUDY: PRE-PAID LEGAL SERVICES, INC., AND THE SEC[28]

Harland C. Stonecipher, chairman and CEO of Pre-Paid Legal Services, Inc. (PPD), couldn't believe the "informal inquiry" letter he received from the SEC suggesting a key element of PPD's accounting did not conform to generally accepted accounting principles (GAAP).

Stonecipher was a seasoned CEO used to challenges, including regulatory matters. Indeed, in 30 short years of doing business, the company that Stonecipher founded to provide middle-income families with affordable quality legal service had faced countless regulatory hurdles in its crusade to revolutionize the delivery of legal services. The SEC was knocking. Stonecipher knew it was time for action and pulled together a team to research this matter and prepare a report for Pre-Paid Legal Services' Board of Directors.

The SEC Asserts That PPD's Accounting for Commission Advances does not Conform to GAAP

The inquiry Pre-Paid Legal Services, Inc., received from the Division of Enforcement of the SEC requesting information related primarily to the company's accounting policies for commission advance receivables from sales associates. The Division of Enforcement's inquiries were informal and did not constitute a formal investigation or proceeding by the SEC. Still, no company in the public arena can long afford a cloud over its accounting.

PPD had long had conservative financial policies, such as no debt and substantial cash reserves. Deloitte & Touche LLP was unequivocal that PPD's accounting for commission advances did conform to GAAP. Clearly, commission advances to associates was complex.

The SEC position seemed firm and potentially very impactful:

1. PPD must change its accounting to conform to SEC recommendations on commission advances to associates.
2. This would amount to a serious cloud over PPD's accounting. At a minimum, the pro forma estimated impact of conforming to SEC specifications would be an immediate and annual decrease for future years in net income, earnings per share (EPS), and total assets as recorded on the company's balance sheet.[29]

The SEC "Choice"

The team debated every angle of the SEC "choice." Pre-Paid Legal Services, Inc., was asked by the SEC to immediately expense all advanced sales commissions and not carry these as assets on the balance sheet. A likely consequence would be a restatement of earnings.

PPD's auditors, Deloitte & Touche, had their best talent on the case and were adamant that the advanced commissions were properly booked, in accordance with GAAP, and were adequately reserved. The auditors disagreed with the SEC and thought the company would be faced with potentially moving well over $100 million in assets off the balance sheet, an unheard of event.

The team debated why the SEC was addressing this matter now with the company. Some believed it was the dramatic growth and success of PPD. There are always those who question success. Others felt it was a combination of several factors in addition to rapid growth: PPD had a unique business model, breaking the traditional mold in the legal field; PPD had a large complex asset, in the form of advanced commissions; and there were inherent concerns by many of multilevel marketing, PPD's principle method of product distribution. Other team members squarely attributed the SEC inquiry directly to press leaks, which involved a combination of predatory short sellers seeking to drive the stock price down for personal gain and the subsequent opportunity for the class-action lawyers to pile on, after the restatement of earnings, claiming fraudulent behavior by PPD.

The Board and CEO Chart a Course

CEO Stonecipher was faced with giving his board the best course of action. His team summarized the pros and cons on following the SEC "choice" to immediately expense all advanced sales commissions and carry none as assets . . . or not.

The Pros of Meeting SEC Requests to Immediately Expense Advanced Commissions

- ▶ Remove a cloud of doubt over their accounting by responding to the SEC request.
- ▶ No negative impact on cash flow. The major asset now placed off balance sheet would push additional earnings into the future quarters for some four to six years.
- ▶ Avoid a potential long-term informal inquiry with the SEC and the related costs.

- Become even more conservative in financial reporting.
- Get on with Pre-Paid Legal Services' business.

The Cons of Meeting SEC Requests to Immediately Expense Advanced Commissions

- Potentially roil the investment community and stock market for PPD shares.
- Move over $100 million in assets off the balance sheet, contrary to advice of Deloitte & Touche.
- Restate financial results for 2 years or more.
- Restatements are magnets for class-action litigation and can scare off investors.
- Decrease net income, earnings per share (EPS), and total assets going forward.

Harland Stonecipher is armed with the facts on the SEC "choice" and is headed into a meeting with Pre-Paid Legal Services' Board of Directors.

The Board of Directors Meets: What Would You Do?

You are a member of the Board of Directors for Pre-Paid Legal Services, Inc. You have the CEO's report and it's time to weigh the options on the SEC "choice": What do you do?

Weigh these options as you make your decision:

1. Do you have sufficient information?
2. Is time of the essence and demanding a quick decision?
3. What is the short- and long-term impact of this decision?

4. Are you ready to make a motion for board action and what is that motion?

5. What would you do if you were CEO Harland Stonecipher?

6. How would you vote as a member of the board?

What Really Happened?

The SEC continued to assert that PPD's accounting for commission advances did not conform to GAAP.[30] Following reasonable appeal efforts, the company changed its accounting to meet SEC specifications. In an extraordinary move, the accounting firm of Deloitte & Touche publicly disagreed with the SEC and stated it would not certify the revised books because they believed they were correct.[31] Given the accounting firm's respectful disagreement with the SEC, they were unable to issue an unqualified audit opinion on the revised financial statements. Deloitte & Touche resigned from the PPD account and the firm Grant Thornton LLP was hired by PPD.[32]

PPD continued to grow rapidly. As expected, the accounting restatement of earnings was very expensive.[33] The stock price, which averaged in the high $20s and low $30s per share for the year 2000, encountered a sharp decline to the $10 per share range in March 2001 and then started a long slow steady climb back to an average price in the $20 per share range in mid-year 2002. The company used the substantial off balance sheet cash flow to fund a stock repurchase plan.

Short sellers remained active and shareholder class-action lawsuits were filed as expected. PPD prospered but was dogged for years by short sellers, those generally critical of multilevel marketing and other SEC matters. In early 2011, PPD announced it would be bought by a prominent New York private equity firm, MidOcean Partners.[34] The offer price was $66.50 per share with a full price of $650 million.[35] The deal closed in mid-2011 and made PPD a private company.

CONCLUSION

CLAIMING YOUR PLACE AT THE BOARDROOM TABLE

Governance is a journey. Congratulations to you for completing the journey through this book. You now have deeper insight and a better road map for achieving excellence in governance and effective directorship, as an individual and as a board member.

If you are seeking to claim your first boardroom seat, I trust you can clearly see the best approach for developing your personal and professional relationships and brand to quickly move into a pool of candidates. If you are a seasoned director, have you identified the next best opportunity for you and quietly spread the word of your interest? Whether you are a rookie or a seasoned director, have you considered how to connect with active directors and CEOs in your community and spheres of influence? I wish you every success with your efforts to soon join your ideal boardroom.

The journey of governance is never-ending. There is always the next hot topic in the field, a new spin on something old, and the occasional, genuinely fresh idea. No matter your experience, when it comes to the theory and practice of good governance, there is always something new to learn. Thanks for your commitment to learning more about boards and governance. May this volume serve you well as a resource.

Today, there is a flood of information on governance that can be overwhelming, especially for busy leaders. Here are a few tips on making the most of pursuing excellence in governance and effective directorship:

▸ **A Few Best Practices.** Keep in mind that best practices are *subjective* and often just *a goal*: subjective in that what is best for others might not be what your board needs; a goal in that a best practice may be something you aspire to, sooner or later, as best fits your board's needs. Best practices are guidelines and one size does *not* fit all. Handle accordingly.

▸ **Consider the Source.** Find the sources and resources that work for you. Governance ideas and proposals come from a range of sources: business groups such as The Conference Board and the Business Roundtable (BRT); regulatory and self-regulatory agencies including the Securities and Exchange Commission (SEC), the New York Stock Exchange (NYSE), and the NASDAQ; groups such as the National Association of Corporate Directors (NACD), the American Bar Association (ABA), and the American Institute of Certified Public Accountants (AICPA); specialty organizations for higher education and health care; and major corporations, especially those vested in good governance including TIAA-CREF and CalPERS. Where do you naturally connect?

▸ **Read Widely.** Governance is an omnipresent topic; you never know where it will arise. The greatest in-your-face reality check for me on CEO and director independence came from reading Walter Isaacson's *Steve Jobs*. Isaacson tells the story of Jobs inviting former SEC chairman Arthur Levitt to join the Apple board, and then withdrawing the offer after reading a speech of Levitt's views on strong director independence. Levitt said Jobs told him, "Frankly, I think some of the issues you raised, while appropriate for some companies, really don't apply to Apple's culture." Levitt wrote, "I was floored that Apple's board is not designed to act independently of the CEO."[1]

Rarely a day goes by when the *Wall Street Journal* does not contain two or three articles on CEO succession, activist shareholders, or other boardroom matters. Top business journals like *Forbes* and *Fortune* frequently highlight major governance matters. Good governance permeates our society and the business world.

If you find a deep passion for governance, read the classics. I've already mentioned how many believe the first breakthrough in America's boardrooms came with a 1992 coup at General Motors. Governance scholars might take you back to another famous lawsuit in American corporate law—an auto case from 1916 involving Henry Ford and the Dodge brothers, John and Horace—known as *Dodge v. Ford Motor Company*. It highlights the current hot topic of shareholder versus stakeholder rights. Also, read a classic book from the early 1930s, which is still in print, called *The Modern Corporation and Private Property* by Adolf A. Berle and Gardiner C. Means. It focuses, in part, on the separation of ownership from control of the modern corporation.

Personally, I read everything written by Ram Charan on governance. He has deep insights from decades of work in boardrooms that have global reach. Likewise, I read everything by William "Bill" George, former chairman and CEO of Medtronic.

▶ **Follow the Major Changes.** Governance occasionally undergoes major changes. Focus on those major shifts. The period immediately following the passage of the Sarbanes-Oxley Act (SOX) of 2002 was a time of intense external regulation. The period after 2008 has seen governance moving beyond external regulation to self-regulation. Today, many boards are positioned for honest assessments of management, are far more willing to deal with unproductive or improper boardroom behavior, and often have a very clear picture of their roles and responsibilities while working in concert with management.

▶ **Continue Your Education.** If you are willing to spend the time, it is fairly easy to stay abreast of major changes in governance. Opportunities for continuing education abound: association programs; university-based programs; programs offered by major law, accounting, and employee benefit firms; programs sponsored by major companies, agencies, search firms, and stock exchanges. The list goes on and on.

There are excellent publications focused on boards, directors, and governance including *NACD Directorship, Directors & Boards, and The Corporate Board,* to name just a few. Even daily e-mails and blogs are available if they fit your interest: "NACD Directors Daily" is my favorite.

▶ **Join the Community and Practice Good Governance.** As you pursue your own role, you will find a community that is generous and regularly willing to share in achieving excellence in governance and effective directorship. Enjoy the journey. I look forward to sharing a conversation with you about your favorite board or governance topic, or meeting you in one of the many boardrooms I visit in my consulting.

Thomas F. Bakewell

Notes

Chapter 1

1. Drucker, Peter. *Management: Tasks, Responsibilities, Practices* (New York: Harper & Row, 1974). Quoted in *BusinessWeek*, July 3, 1989.
2. http://www.census.gov/econ/smallbus.html.
3. www.creditriskmonitor.com; http://nccs.urban.org/statistics/quick facts.cfm.
4. 2012–2013 NACD Private Company Governance Survey.
5. Kelly Greene, "Boomers on Board," *Wall Street Journal* Spring 2013.
6. 2012–2013 NACD Nonprofit Governance Survey, p. 5.
7. *Spencer Stuart Board Index 2012.*
8. "Tales from the Frontlines." *Wall Street Journal,* April 11, 2011. http://online.wsj.com/news/articles/SB10001424052748704101604576246773120528078.
9. Ms. Wilderotter, chairman and CEO of Frontier Communications and a director at Procter & Gamble and Xerox, spoke at the 2013 NACD Annual Conference along with Robert "Bob" Hallagan, the vice president and managing director of Korn/Ferry International. Wilderotter is also the author of the article "How to Get on a Board," *Bloomberg BusinessWeek*, April 11, 2013.

Chapter 2

1. *Hampshire Group, Ltd. v. Kuttner,* CIV.A. 3607-VCS, 2010 WL 2739995 (Del. Ch. July 12, 2010).
2. http://dictionary.reference.com/browse/fiduciary.

3. *Stegemeier v. Magness*, 728 A.2d 557, 562 (Del. 1999).

4. *Black's Law Dictionary*, 7th ed. (Eagan, MN: West Publishing Corporation, 1999), 523, 640.

5. See, for example, Harry G. Henn, *Handbook of the Law of Corporations and Other Business Entities*, 2nd ed. (Eagan, MN: West Publishing Company, 1970), 457–458.

6. Millstein, Gregory, et al. "Fiduciary Duties Under U.S. Law," American Bar Association, footnote 14 and p. 4.

7. http://www.cnbc.com/id/100862219.

8. http://www.sec.gov/about/whatwedo.shtml.

9. 2012–2013 NACD Public Company Governance Survey.

10. Jeffrey A. Sonnenfeld, "What Makes Great Boards Great," *Harvard Business Review*, September 2002, 80(9):106–113, 126.

11. Richard J. Connors, *Warren Buffett on Business: Principles from the Sage of Omaha* (Hoboken, NJ: Wiley, 2010), 17, 25.

12. Connors, *Warren Buffett on Business*, 18–19.

13. Connors, *Warren Buffett on Business*, 22.

14. Connors, *Warren Buffett on Business*, 20, 24.

15. Connors, *Warren Buffett on Business*, 20–21.

16. *CEO Succession Practices: 2013 Edition*, The Conference Board Report.

17. The *Spencer Stuart Board Index 2012*.

18. https://www.sec.gov/rules/final/33-8220.htm#audit.

19. http://www.pwc.com/us/en/corporate-governance/whistleblower -bounty-program.jhtml.

20. http://www.investopedia.com/terms/i/independentauditor.asp.

21. http://www.investopedia.com/terms/r/related-partytransaction.asp.

22. http://articles.philly.com/1990-05-13/business/25886372_1_law -firms-reading-anthracite-referral-fees.

23. http://www.inman.com/2006/09/07/hud-settles-kickback-cases -new-england-attorney-appraiser/.

24. *Black's Law Dictionary*, 7th ed. (Eagan, MN: West Publishing Corporation, 1999).

25. *VonFeldtv. Stifel Financial Corp.*, 714 A.2d 79, 84 (Del. 1998) (en banc).

26. Disclosure of Commission Position on Indemnification for Securities Act Liabilities, 17 C.F.R. §§ 229.510.

27. *Globus v. Law Research Serv., Inc.*, 418 F.2d 1276, 1288 (2d Cir. 1969).

28. http://www.insurancejournal.com/news/national/2011/02/28/ 188339.htm.

29. The words "Don't Be Sleazy, Don't Be Sloppy" are provided compliments of Professor Charles Elson, University of Delaware, in his Stella lecture "Fiduciary Duties of Corporate Boards for the National Association of Corporate Directors as presented in their foundation course for new corporate directors, NACI Director Professionalism*, a two-day course that teaches the fundamentals of boardroom effectiveness.

CHAPTER 3

1. 2013–2014 NACD Public Company Governance Survey.

2. Sections 163 and 164 of the *New York Stock Exchange Listed Company Manual*, Section 303A.09. Section 164 includes Website Posting Requirements and Disclosure Requirements.

3. Boris Feldman is a member of Wilson Sonsini Goodrich & Rosati, in Palo Alto, California.

4. http://paygovernance.com/chapter-6-compensation-committee-responsibilities-and-best-practices/

5. http://www.businessroundtable.org/sites/default/files/Business%20 Roundtable%20Nominating%20Committee%20Principles.pdf

6. 2014 JPMorgan Chase & Co. Board Committee from website.

7. 2014 Board of Visitors' Executive Committee, Board of Visitors, University of Virginia website.

8. *Corporate Board Minutes: A Director's Guide, NACD 2013*. For those interested in knowing more about the art of handling boardroom minutes, I recommend: a short five-page article that is highly practice-oriented and I consider it a classic titled "Making Board Minutes Count" by M. Boone, G. Samuel, and T. Wilson, *NACD-Directors Monthly*, October 2007, and a 28-page publication titled *Corporate Board Minutes: A Director's Guide, NACD 2013*. The NACD acknowledges The Society of Corporate Secretaries and Governance Professionals for support in this publication and the Society is a great resource for those wanting to go even deeper into minutes and many other important corporate secretaries duties (www.governance professionals.org).

9. Cornelis A. de Kluyver, *A Primer on Corporate Governance* (New York: Business Expert Press, 2009), 58.

10. BoardSource Nonprofit Governance Index 2010, 19. Published by BoardSource and available on their website, www.boardsource.org.

11. Adam Epstein. *The Perfect Corporate Board: A Handbook for Mastering the Unique Challenges of Small-Cap Companies* (New York: McGraw-Hill, 2012).

12. The New Era case study was written by Tom Bakewell for the National Association of Corporate Directors and has been used in its foundation course for new corporate directors, NACD Director Professionalism*, a two-day course that teaches the fundamentals of boardroom effectiveness.

CHAPTER 4

1. http://www.investopedia.com/terms/i/internalcontrols.asp.

2. Donald R. Cressey, *Other People's Money: A Study in the Social Psychology of Embezzlement* (Montclair, NJ: Patterson Smith, 1973).

3. http://www.inquisitr.com/222444/rita-crundell-illinois-comptroller -allegedly-embezzled-30-million-to-fund-horse-breeding-business/.

4. http://www.nydailynews.com/news/national/ex-bookkeeper -20-years-stealing-53-million-article-1.1264369.

5. http://www.bizjournals.com/twincities/blog/law/2013/10/ cliftonlarsonallen-dixon-lawsuit-settled.html.

6. http://www.reuters.com/article/2014/01/21/mfglobal-cftc-idUSL2 N0KV0ZC20140121.

7. *Ibid.*

8. http://www.reuters.com/article/2014/02/11/us-mfglobal-corzine-id USBREA1A1QS20140211.

9. http://www.coso.org/aboutus.htm.

10. http://www.coso.org/ic.htm.

11. J. Stephen McNally, CPA, *The 2013 COSO Framework & SOX Compliance: One Approach to an Effective Transition* (Montvale, NJ: IMA The Association of Accountants and Financial Professionals in Business, Strategic Finance, June 2013), figure from page 4.

12. http://www.coso.org/audit_shop.htm.

13. http://ww2.cfo.com/accounting-tax/2006/03/the-trouble-with-coso/ view-all/; Helen Shaw, "The Trouble with COSO," *CFO Magazine* (March 15, 2006).

14. http://www.ecfr.gov/cgi-bin/text-idx?c=ecfr&rgn=div5&view=text&node=17:2.0.1.1.11&idno=17#17:2.0.1.1.11.4.35.3.

15. Ken Tysiac, "Nine tips for effective MD&A reporting," *Journal of Accountancy* (Dec. 4, 2012). (referencing presentation of Brian Lane of the law firm Gibson, Dunn &Crutcher) http://www.journal ofaccountancy.com/News/20126936.htm.

16. http://www.sec.gov/rules/final/2006/33-8765.pdf.

17. http://www.sec.gov/rules/proposed/33-8655.pdf.

18. http://www.sec.gov/rules/proposed/33-8655.pdf.

19. Figure 4.6, "How to Read a Financial Statement in Plain English," on pages 160–161, provides basic guidelines and tips for reading the key reports and schedules in financial statements. It applies to the financial schedules found in this chapter, in other chapters, and in most if not all of the boardrooms you enter.

20. 15 U.S.C. §§78dd-1(a), 78dd-2(a), 78dd-3(a).

21. H.R. Conf. Rep. No. 100-579, at 919–20 (1988).

22. http:www.bloomberg.com/news/2014-01-07/jpmorgan-to-pay -2-6-billion-over-madoff-lapses.html, Patricia Hurtado, Greg Farrell, and Hugh Son, "JP Morgan to Pay $2.6 Billion over Madoff Scheme Lapses," *Bloomberg News Online* (Jan. 8, 2014).

23. http://www.fbi.gov/newyork/press-releases/2014/chairman-cfo-and -executive-director-of-dewey-leboeuf-indicted-on-grand-larceny -fraud-charges.

24. http://online.wsj.com/news/articles/SB100014240527023036495045 7 7498213432505428; Juro Osawa, "Olympus Faces Setback in Court," *Wall Street Journal Online* (June 30, 2012).

25. https://www.tshaonline.org/handbook/online/articles/doe08.

26. http://content.time.com/time/business/article/0,8599,201871,00.html.

27. http://content.time.com/time/specials/packages/article/ 0,28804,2009445_2009447_2009502,00.html.

28. https://www.tshaonline.org/handbook/online/articles/doe08.

29. http://money.cnn.com/2006/10/23/news/newsmakers/skilling_sentence/.

30. http://www.eoionline.org/wp/wp-content/uploads/social-security/ AfterEnronPensionReformProposals-Mar02.pdf.

31. http://www.forbes.com/sites/robertwood/2012/09/11/ubs-bradley -birkenfeld-gets-104-million-blows-doors-off-irs-whistleblower

-program/ and Robert W. Wood, "UBS" Bradley Birkenfeld Gets $104 Million, Blows Door Off IRS Whistleblower Program (Sept. 11, 2012).

32. http://online.wsj.com/news/articles/SB100008723963904440175045776 45412614237708; and Laura Saunders and Robin Sidel, "Whistle blower Gets $104 Million," *Wall Street Journal Online* (September 11, 2012).

33. http://www.lexisnexis.com/legalnewsroom/labor-employment/b/labor -employment-top-blogs/archive/2013/04/03/3-5-million-federal-jury -award-in-whistleblower-wrongful-termination-case.aspx.

CHAPTER 5

1. *Report of the NACD Blue Ribbon Commission on Board-Shareholder Communications* (Washington, D.C., National Association of Corporate Directors, 2008).

2. Elizabeth Mullen. "Board and Shareholder Communications," National Association of Corporate Directors Online, posted October 16, 2012, http://blog.nacdonline.org/2012/10/board-and -shareholder-communications/

3. Jeffrey D. Morgan, "Board-Shareholder Engagement Survey—2013 Report," National Investor Relations Institute, posted 2014, http://www .niri.org/Main-Menu-Category/resource/publications/Executive-Alert/ Board-Shareholder-Engagement–2013-Survey-Results-102513.aspx

4. *Report of the NACD Blue Ribbon Commission on Board-Shareholder Communications* (Washington, D.C.: National Association of Corporate Directors, 2008).

5. Frederick D. Lipman and L. Keith Lipman, *Corporate Governance Best Practices: Strategies for Public, Private, and Not-for-Profit Organizations* (Hoboken, NJ: John Wiley & Sons, 2006).

6. *Report of the NACD Blue Ribbon Commission on Board-Shareholder Communications* (Washington, D.C.: National Association of Corporate Directors, 2008).

7. Deborah S. Birnbach, R. Todd Cronan, Lisa R. Haddad, and Michael T. Jones, "SEC Clarifies Social Media Use and Reg FD Compliance," Goodwin Procter LLP, April 5, 2013, http://www.goodwinprocter.com/ Publications/Newsletters/Client-Alert/2013/0405_SEC-Clarifies -Social-Media-Use-and-Reg-FD-Compliance.aspx?article=1.

8. Michele Hooper and Anne Simpson, "How to Engage Shareholders When Selecting New Directors," NACD Directorship, posted January 15, 2013, http://www.directorship.com/how-to-engage -shareholders-when-selecting-new-directors/print/.

9. Definitions of "security": (1) An investment instrument, other than an insurance policy or fixed annuity, issued by a corporation, government, or other organization which offers evidence of debt or equity (http://www.investorwords.com/4446/security.html); (2) A financing or investment instrument issued by a company or government agency that denotes an ownership interest and provides evidence of a debt, a right to share in the earnings of the issuer, or a right in the distribution of a property (http://www.businessdictionary.com/ definition/security.html).

10. http://www.sec.gov/about/whatwedo.shtml.

11. http://www.sec.gov/about/whatwedo.shtml.

12. http://www.sec.gov/about/whatwedo.shtml.

13. http://www.forbes.com/2002/03/22/0322enronpay.html.

14. http://www.forbes.com/sites/realspin/2013/12/09/former-tyco-ceo -dennis-kozlowski-was-one-of-the-great-all-time-value-creators/.

15. http://www.reuters.com/article/2012/06/14/us-tyco-curtain-idUS BRE85D1M620120614.

16. http://online.wsj.com/news/articles/SB1027516262583067680.

17. http://www.ey.com/US/en/Issues/Governance-and-reporting/SOX-1.

18. http://www.gpo.gov/fdsys/pkg/PPP-2002-book2/html/PPP-2002 -book2-doc-pg1319.htm.

19. http://online.wsj.com/article/SB1010695966620300040.html?dsk=y.

20. http://www.fasab.gov/accounting-standards/authoritative-source-of -gaap/accounting-standards/fasab-handbook/20.

21. http://www.fasb.org/jsp/FASB/Page/SectionPage&cid=1176156304264.

22. Andreas M. Fleckner, "FASB and IASB: Dependence Despite Independence," Virginia Law & Business Review 3, no. 2 (Fall 2008): 282.

23. http://www.fasb.org/jsp/FASB/Page/SectionPage&cid=1176156304264.

24. Andreas M. Fleckner, "FASB and IASB: Dependence Despite Independence," Virginia Law & Business Review 3, no. 2 (Fall 2008): 280.

25. http://pcaobus.org/NEWS/Pages/default.aspx.

26. Nancy T. Hill, John McEnroe, and Kevin T. Stevens, "Auditors' Reactions to Sarbanes-Oxley and the PCAOB," *CPA Journal Online*, November 5, 2005, http://www.nysscpa.org/cpajour.nal/2005/1105/special_issue/essentials/p32.htm; see also www.sarbanes-oxley-act .bix/SarbanesOxleySection 101.htm.

27. www.sarbanes-oxley-act.bix/SarbanesOxleySection 101.htm.

28. James K. Glassman and J.W. Verret, "How to Fix Our Broken Proxy Advisory System," Mercatus Center, George Mason University, April 16, 2013, http://mercatus.org/publication/how-fix-our-broken -proxy-advisory-system.

29. Ryan Vlastelica, "Apple buyback burnishes earnings per share, may soothe critics," *Reuters U.S. Edition*, February 7, 2014, http://www.reuters .com/article/2014/02/07/us-apple-icahn-idUSBREA161GA20140207.

30. Arik Hesseldahl, "Two More Proxy Firms Back the $24.4 Billion Dell Buyout Plan," *All Things Digital* Online, July 8, 2013, http:// allthingsd.com/20130708/two-more-proxy-firms-back-the-24-4 -billion-dell-buyout-plan/.

31. http://www.ft.com/intl/cms/s/0/12d1234a-b718-11e2-a249 -00144feabdc0.html#axzz2sxzutWa3.

32. Steve Daniels, "Shareholders urged to vote James Crown off JPMorgan board," *Crain's Chicago Business*, May 6, 2013, http://www.chicagobusiness .com/article/20130506/NEWS01/130509839/shareholders-urged-to -vote-james-crown-off-jpmorgan-board.

33. http://online.wsj.com/news/articles/SB100014241278873238997045 78587421635869116.

34. http://www.bloomberg.com/news/2010-11-04/dynegy-takeover-by -blackstone-opposed-by-proxy-firm-glass-lewis.html.

35. Sheryl Gay Stolberg and Bill Vlasic, "U.S. Lays Down Terms for Auto Bailout," *New York Times*, March 30, 2009, http://www.nytimes .com/2009/03/30/business/30auto.html.

36. David Welch, "Ed Whitacre's Battle to Save GM from Itself," *Bloomberg BusinessWeek*, April 29, 2010, http://www.businessweek .com/magazine/content/10_19/b4177048204431.htm.

37. Ed Whitacre with Leslie Cauley, *American Turnaround: Reinventing AT&T and GM and the Way We Do Business in the USA* (New York: BusinessPlus, 2013).

CHAPTER 6

1. http://www.forbes.com/profile/david-pottruck-1/.
2. Andrea Redmond and Patricia Crisafulli, *Comebacks: Powerful Lessons from Leaders Who Endured Setbacks and Recaptured Success on Their Terms* (San Francisco: Jossey-Bass, 2010), 88.
3. Judith Dobrzynski, "Board Members, Too, Are Getting Investor Scrutiny," *New York Times*, March 12, 1996.
4. Nick Summers, "Jamie Dimon Wins Big in JPMorgan Shareholder Vote," *Bloomberg BusinessWeek Online*, May 21, 2013, http://www .businessweek.com/articles/2013-05-21/jamie-dimon-wins-big-in -jpmorgan-shareholder-vote.
5. http://www.jonesday.com/files/Publication/aa3be3e4-0364-4d7a -80bb-022a02591ed0/Presentation/PublicationAttachment/c90eabda -76c3-408d-a888-108fea665f10/Kopes%26RodmanPDF2Q06.pdf.
6. *CNBC* interview with Jeffrey Sonnenfeld, May 2013.
7. http://www.ifac.org/sites/default/files/publications/files/IGPG -Evaluating-and-Improving-Governance.pdf.
8. Beverly Behan, *Great Companies Deserve Great Boards: A CEO's Guide to the Boardroom* (New York: Palgrave Macmillan, 2011).
9. Jeffrey M. Stein and Laura Oleck Hewett, "Key Issues in Board Self-Evaluations," *Boardroom Briefing: The Legal Issue 2008*, http://apps .kslaw.com/Library/publication/D&BBB_Fall08_SteinHewett.pdf.
10. Robert H. Hallagan and B. Kenneth West, "Board Evaluation: Improving Director Effectiveness," *NACD Director's Monthly*, December 2012.
11. http://www.tenethealth.com/about/pages/default.aspx.
12. http://www.tenethealth.com/about/pages/missionandvalues.aspx.
13. http://www.tenethealth.com/about/pages/corporategovernance.aspx.
14. http://www.tenethealth.com/About/pages/boardofdirectors.aspx.
15. http://www.tenethealth.com/about/pages/corporategovernance.aspx.
16. http://www.tenethealth.com/about/pages/corporategovernance.aspx.
17. http://www.tenethealth.com/about/pages/corporategovernance.aspx.
18. http://www.tenethealth.com/about/pages/corporategovernance.aspx.
19. http://www.tenethealth.com/about/pages/corporategovernance.aspx.
20. http://www.tenethealth.com/about/pages/corporategovernance .aspx.

21. Ram Charan, "Ending the CEO Succession Crisis," *Harvard Business Review*, February 2005, http://hbr.org/2005/02/ending-the-ceo -succession-crisis/ar/1.

22. http://www.weil.com/files/upload/Practical_Law_Feb_2012.pdf.

23. Thomas Saporito and Paul Winum, *Inside CEO Succession* (San Francisco: Jossey-Bass, 2012), 39.

24. Ram Charan, "Ending the CEO Succession Crisis," *Harvard Business Review*, February 2005, http://hbr.org/2005/02/ending-the-ceo -succession-crisis/ar/1.

25. *Ibid.*

26. *Ibid.*

27. Yet another survey, however, found that from 2000 to 2010, outsiders failed at a rate of almost twice that compared to insiders. Booz Allen Hamilton, *CEO Succession Survey*, 2010.

28. James M. Citrin and Dayton Ogden, "Succeeding at Succession," *Harvard Business Review*, November 2010, 29–31, http://hbr .org/2010/11/succeeding-at-succession/ar/1

29. *Ibid.*

30. Ram Charan, "Ending the CEO Succession Crisis," *Harvard Business Review*, February 2005, http://hbr.org/2005/02/ending-the-ceo -succession-crisis/ar/1.

31. David A. Nadler, Beverly A. Behan, and Mark B. Nadler, *Building Better Boards: A Blueprint for Effective Governance* (San Francisco: Jossey-Bass, 2006).

32. http://corporate.ford.com/doc/2006_AR.pdf, p. 2.

33. http://corporate.ford.com/doc/2006_AR.pdf, p. 5.

34. This section draws on an April 25, 2013 NACD Heartland Chapter presentation by Irvine O. Hockaday, Jr., regarding his time as Ford's lead director of the board during a CEO search that resulted in the eventual hiring of Alan Mullaly. Conversations with Mr. Hockaday and numerous books and articles including Kate Linebaugh, "Designated Driver: Ford Taps Boeing Executive as CEO," *Wall Street Journal*, September 6, 2006; Bryce G. Hoffman, *American Icon: Alan Mullaly and the Fight to Save Ford Motor Company* (New York: Random House, 2012); and Ram Charan, Dennis Carey, and Michael Useem, *Boards That Lead* (Boston: Harvard Business Review Press, 2014), 105–109.

CHAPTER 7

1. Carl Icahn, "Carl Icahn: What I Do Is Good For America," *Forbes*, June 24, 2013, p. 18. www.forbes.com/sites/stevenbertoni /2013/06/06/carl-icahn-what-i-do-is-good-for-america/.

2. David Benoit and Emily Glazer, "Ackman Defends Record, Says May Choose to Exit Penney," *Wall Street Journal*, Aug. 21, 2013, http://blogs.wsj.com/moneybeat/2013/08/21/ackman-defends-track -record-herbalife-position-in-letter-to-investors/.

3. Svea Herbst-Bayliss, "Ackman's mettle tested as Herbalife battle rolls into year two," *Reuters U.S. Edition Online*, December 20, 2013, http://www.reuters.com/article/2013/12/20/us-hedgefunds-ackman -idUSBRE9BJ1B320131220

4. http://www.rillc.com/about.htm.

5. Francesco Guerrera and James Politi, "The Lone Ranger of Boardroom Battles," *Financial Times*, February 25, 2008, www.rillc .com/news/20080225_RalphWhitworthLoneRanger.pdf.

6. WSJ Blogs, *Deal Journal*, "Meet H-P's New Chairman: Activist Ralph Whitworth," April 4, 2013.

7. Carl Icahn, Letter of Welcome, received automatically on June 30, 2014 via email following registration at www.shareholders squaretable.com.

8. www.streetinsider.com/Hedge+Funds/Carl+Icahn+Letter+to +Apples+(AAPL)+Tim+Cook/8807386.html.

9. *Ibid.*

10. Henry Blodget, "If Apple Followed Carl Icahn's Advice, It Would Be Strapping A Dead Elephant To Its Back," *Business Insider*, October 29, 2013, http://www.businessinsider.com/apple-carl-icahn-2013 -10#ixzz2obiG23c.

11. www.longleafpartners.com/about_us.

12. "Letter to Our Shareholders," Longleaf Partners Funds, Quarterly Report 1Q 2013, pp. 2–3, http://longleafpartners.com/sites/default/ files/commentary/Shareholder Letter-2013-1Q.pdf.

13. *Ibid.*

14. *Ibid.*

15. *Ibid.*

16. "Letter To Our Shareholders," Longleaf Partners Funds, Quarterly Report 3Q 2012, pp. 3–4, http://longleafpartners.com/sites/default/files/commentary/ShareLettersTo1Q2014.pdf.

17. Adam Wilmoth, "Chesapeake names new chairman: Chesapeake Energy Corp. named five new directors on Thursday," *NewsOK*, June 21, 2012, http://newsok.com/chesapeake-names-new-chairman/article/3686371.

18. "Letter to Our Shareholders," Longleaf Partners Funds, Quarterly Report 3Q 2013, p. 2, http: //longleafpartners.com/sites/default/files/commentary/Shareholder Letter-2013-3Q.pdf.

19. www.dell.com/learn/us/en/uscorp1/about-dell-investor.

20. "Letter to Our Shareholders," Longleaf Partners Funds, Annual Report 4Q 2011, p. 2, http://longleafpartners.com/sites/default/files/commentary/ShareLettersTo1Q2014.pdf.

21. Arik Hesseldahl, "Dell's Go-Private Case Emerged as Business Eroded," *All Things Digital*, March 29, 2013, http://allthingsd.com/20130329/dells-go-private-case-emerged-as-business-eroded/.

22. "Letter To Our Shareholders," Longleaf Partners Funds, Quarterly Report 3Q 2013, p. 2, http://longleafpartners.com/sites/default/files/commentary/Shareholder Letter-2013-3Q.pdf.

23. http://www.sec.gov/Archives/edgar/data/826083/000092166913000029/dellexhibit19913.htm.

24. http://www.cnbc.com/id/101377530; Jennifer Ablan, "Icahn gives up Apple buyback plan after ISS urges 'no' vote," *Reuters U.S. Edition Online*, February 10, 2014, http://www.reuters.com/article/2014/02/10/us-apple-icahn-idUSBREA1913T20140210.

25. Michael J. De La Merced, "I.S.S. Sides With Apple Against Icahn," *Dealbook*, February 9, 2014, http://dealbook.nytimes.com/2014/02/09/i-s-s-sides-with-apple-in-battle-against-icahn/?_php=true&_type=blogs&_r=0.

26. *Ibid.*

27. Walter Hamilton, "Carl Icahn to get three more seats on Herbalife board," *Los Angeles Times Business Online*, March 24, 2014, http://www.latimes.com/business/money/la-fi-mo-carl-icahn-to-get-three-more-seats-on-herbalife-board-20140324,0,3587283.story#axzz2ytawRkGX.

28. This Pre-Paid Legal Services, Inc. case study was prepared based on actual facts involving PPD as developed from research and provided by founder, Chairman and CEO Harland Stonecipher. The case was discussed with, reviewed, and approved by Stonecipher. The Board of Directors meeting scenario and questions are provided for discussion related to good governance and for teaching purposes.

29. *McNamara v. Pre-Paid Leg. Services, Inc.*, 189 Fed. Appx. 702, 707-08 (10th Cir. 2006, unpublished); *Deloitte &Touche LLP Statement Regarding the Decision By Pre-Paid Legal Services, Inc. and Deloitte & Touche To End Their Relationship as Client and Auditor*, Aug. 1, 2001, http://www.thefreelibrary.com/Deloitte+%26+Touche+LLP+Statement+Regarding+the+Decision+By+Pre-Paid...-a076913039.

30. Stephen Taub, "Pre-Paid Legal Expects Big Hit from Earnings Restatement," May 17, 2001, http://www.cfo.com/printable/article.cfm/2995370.

31. Jonathan D. Glater and Floyd Norris, "Deloitte Parts With S.E.C. Over Audit of Company," *New York Times*, August 2, 2001, www.nytimes.com/2001/08/02/business/deloitte-parts-with-sec-over-audit-of-company.html.

32. Melissa Davis, "Deloitte & Touche quits as Pre-Paid Legal auditor," Aug. 3, 2001, http://newsok.com/deloitte-touche-quits-as-pre-paid-legal-auditor/article/2750343.

33. "Company News; Restatement by Pre-Paid Legal Reduces Earnings," *New York Times*, August 1, 2001.

34. M. Scott Carter, "Pre-Paid Legal Sold for $650M," *The Journal Record*, January 31, 2011, http://journalrecord.com/2011/01/31/pre-paid-legal-confirms-650-million-buyout-finance/.

35. "Pre-Paid Legal in $650 Million Buyout," Jan. 31, 2001, http://dealbook.nytimes.com/2011/01/31/pre-paid-legal-in-650-million-buyout/?_php=true&_type=blogs&_r=0.

CONCLUSION

1. Walter Isaacson, *Steve Jobs* (New York: Simon & Schuster, 2011), 321.

INDEX

ABOUT THE AUTHORS

Thomas F. Bakewell, JD, CPA, is an experienced director and business advisor to CEOs and boards on strategy, governance, and transformation. As a Board Leadership Fellow and faculty member with the National Association of Corporate Directors (NACD), Mr. Bakewell speaks on diverse governance topics including: handling conflicts of interest, director misconduct, building productive boards, managing crisis, developing private company boards, and non-profit board success. He leads board retreats and strategic planning, especially when it is not business as usual, and regularly facilitates crucial boardroom conversations. His specialty is boardroom transitions and developing renewed boardroom strategies. Prior to his advisory practice, Mr. Bakewell was Senior Vice President, Law and Director of Financial Planning in forming one of the nation's largest health care systems. He is an attorney and a certified public accountant.

James J. Darazsdi, CPA, CMA, Ph.D., had an extensive career both practicing and teaching the principles of good corporate governance and risk oversight. Past chairman of the National Association of Corporate Directors (NACD) and past CEO of Rocco Inc., he served on more than 25 boards, including Perdue Farms Inc., Hyde Manufacturing Company, Inc., High Industries Inc., and Interstate Resources, Inc. Dr. Darazsdi's academic appointments included President of Nichols College, executive in residence at Washington College, and executive in residence at Jacksonville University. He also served on the faculty of NACD, offering programs in the United States and throughout the world in conjunction with the International Finance Corporation (IFC) and The World Bank.